Bob Wilson's Ultimate Collection of Peculiar Sporting Lingo

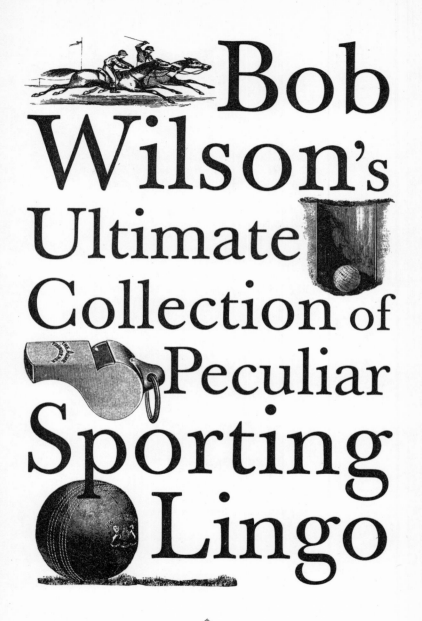

Bob Wilson's Ultimate Collection of Peculiar Sporting Lingo

ICON BOOKS

Published in the UK in 2008 by
Icon Books Ltd, The Old Dairy,
Brook Road, Thriplow,
Cambridge SG8 7RG
email: info@iconbooks.co.uk
www.iconbooks.co.uk

Parts of this book were previously published by Icon Books
in 2006 under the title *Googlies, Nutmegs & Bogeys* and
in 2007 under the title *Rucks, Pucks & Sliders*

Sold in the UK, Europe, South Africa and Asia by
Faber & Faber Ltd, 3 Queen Square,
London WC1N 3AU
or their agents

Distributed in the UK, Europe, South Africa and Asia by
TBS Ltd, TBS Distribution Centre, Colchester Road,
Frating Green, Colchester CO7 7DW

Published in Australia in 2008 by
Allen & Unwin Pty Ltd,
PO Box 8500, 83 Alexander Street,
Crows Nest, NSW 2065

Distributed in Canada by
Penguin Books Canada,
90 Eglinton Avenue East, Suite 700,
Toronto, Ontario M4P 2YE

ISBN: 978-184831-002-5

Typesetting and design by Simmons Pugh

Printed and bound in the UK by Clays of Bungay

About the author

Born in Chesterfield, Bob Wilson found success playing in goal at school and gained England schoolboy honours in 1957. After qualifying as a physical education teacher at Loughborough College, he signed for Arsenal in 1963. He made more than 300 first-team appearances, helping the Gunners win the European Fairs Cup in 1970 and, one year later, the coveted League Championship and FA Cup 'double'. He also became the first English-born player to be capped for Scotland.

In 1974, he embarked on a second career in sports journalism for BBC Television. He presented *Football Focus* for twenty years and was also a regular presenter of *Match of the Day*, *Grandstand*, *Sportsnight* and *Breakfast News Sport*. In August 1994, he was lured to the rival channel to be ITV's main football presenter.

An FA Full Badge Coach since 1967, he specialised in the coaching of goalkeepers for 28 years. During that time, the goalkeepers at Arsenal, Queens Park Rangers, Southampton, Tottenham and Luton benefited from his training methods. He ran his own Goalkeeping School for youngsters from 1982 until 1995. He coached the keepers at Arsenal including Pat Jennings and David Seaman.

He was Chairman of the London Football Coaches Association between 1988 and 2007. In 1989, he was awarded an honorary degree by Loughborough University for services to football. In 1997 he was appointed to the Board of Governors of the University of Hertfordshire. More recently, he was awarded honorary doctorates by the University of Derby in 2000 and Middlesex University in 2004.

He has written many books on football, mainly involving goalkeeping. These include his history of goalkeeping, *You've Got To Be Crazy* (1989), and his autobiography, *Behind the Network* (2003).

He was awarded an OBE in 2007 for services to his charity, the Willow Foundation (see page 21), which he and his wife Megs founded in August 1999, in memory of their daughter Anna who died in December 1998. Bob and Megs have two sons: John, a radio journalist, and Robert, a photographer.

CONTENTS

~ Contents ~

~ Contents ~

~ Contents ~

~ Contents ~

~ Contents ~

~ Contents ~

The Willow Foundation

Royalties from the sale of this book will go to the Willow Foundation.

This Foundation is a national charity dedicated to providing quality of life and quality of time for seriously ill young adults (aged 16–40) through the provision of special days. The Foundation defines seriously ill as any condition that is life-threatening. To date, special days have been organised for young adults living with, among other conditions: cancer, motor neurone disease, cystic fibrosis, heart disease, organ failure and muscular dystrophy. The aim of any special day is to offer time out from treatment and allow seriously ill young adults to spend quality time with friends and/or family while pursuing an activity they all enjoy. Each special day is entirely of the applicant's choosing and is organised in meticulous detail. The Foundation funds every aspect of the chosen special day. For some, a special day is their last chance to fulfil a dream. For others, it is the opportunity to return some normality back into their lives. But for all, a special day creates precious memories for the future. Established by former Arsenal and Scotland goalkeeper and TV presenter, Bob Wilson, and his wife Megs, the Willow Foundation is a lasting memorial to their daughter, Anna, who died of cancer aged 31.

To find out more about the charity please go to: www.willowfoundation.org.uk

Introduction

For as long as I can recall, sport has featured in my life – whether simply as a hobby and interest, or as my chosen profession. I come from a sporting family, my Scottish dad being an accomplished cricketer, golfer and footballer, in that order. My four brothers and one sister all found a sport or sports in which they achieved success. Like me they also learned that, as in life, you win, lose or draw along the way, accompanied by huge ups and downs, laughter and tears. I was nicknamed 'Supergame-Rottengame', such were my mood swings following victory and defeat.

Once my dad had, more or less, ordered me to get a 'proper job first' rather than allow me to sign professional forms for Manchester United, I turned to Loughborough College, the leading seat of Sports Education in the country. As soon as I'd qualified as a sports teacher, I rekindled my ambition to play football at the highest level. Arsenal FC became my home and for twelve years as goalkeeper and 28 years as a specialised goalkeeping coach my hunger for success was nourished. After my football-playing career had ended, and alongside my coaching, I was lucky enough to become the first professional sportsman to present all of BBC TV's major sports programmes – *Grandstand*,

Sportsnight and *Match of the Day* – as well as World Cup finals and the Olympic Games.

So a combination of necessity, enthusiasm and love has ensured a pretty firm grasp of sporting terminology over the years. Nevertheless, it always occurred to me that I had little or no idea as to how much of it had been conceived or evolved. When I first had the idea of unravelling the origins of the language I never anticipated the variety of reactions that it would inspire, both for me exploring the derivations and then from those to whom I had the pleasure in relaying the stories, before I committed my pen to paper. Basically, I hope that the hundreds of funny, obscure and often downright bizarre terms from the sporting world in this book will provoke a similar level of incredulity, shock, disbelief and laughter on discovery of their origins.

The book is a compilation of my two previous explorations of the subject: *Googlies, Nutmegs & Bogeys* and *Rucks, Pucks & Sliders*, but I have added a whole new batch of entries to make what I believe is the most comprehensive guide to the origins of sporting terminology ever compiled. I very much hope that all sporting fans will enjoy having this collection within their library. Perhaps it may prove valuable to sports presenters nationwide who often find themselves with time to fill on air, or even challenged by guests or the public to explain how a saying came about. I know I would have appreciated such a book during my 28 years with the BBC and ITV.

Above all, this compilation carries on from the two original books in helping to raise funds for the Willow Foundation. Every book sold means increased revenue for the charity and with it the possibility of giving more and more special days for seriously ill young adults between the ages 16–40.

Thank you on behalf of those individuals, their families and friends and all of those who work at the charity. It's appropriate that, in this book of terminology, I explain the origins of 'Willow' in this context. It started off as my nickname during my footballing days at Arsenal, based on the name Wilson. My goalkeeping ensured I was called lots of other names as well.

However, our daughter Anna became known as 'Wills' and 'Willow', a nickname given to her by her husband Mitchell Carey. It was during her challenging five-year journey with cancer that Anna taught us the value of having a special day to look forward to, a day that provided excitement when illness and treatment made such normality difficult in the extreme.

As a tribute and in memory of Anna's vision, it was decided that this unique charity, in a previously disregarded age group of 16–40, should bear her moniker and be called the Willow Foundation.

Addicks

[football] – *a nickname for Charlton Athletic FC*

Some believe that this name is simply a corruption of *Athletic*, although the more popular and likely theory is that it derives from the word *haddock*; the club was formed by a group of teenagers in 1905 and sponsored in its early years by a local fish-monger named Arthur Bryan, while they settled at their ground, the Valley. After matches, he would give both the home and away teams a fish supper. The story goes that if Charlton lost, they would have cod, but if they won, they would dine on the more expensive *'addock*, which then produced the nickname *Addicks*.

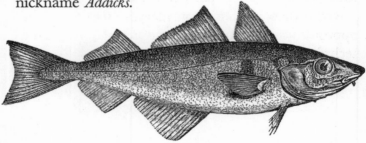

agricultural

[cricket] – *an adjective used to describe an elaborate heave at the ball or similar shot that wouldn't necessarily be found in the average coaching manual*

More often than not this is used to describe a shot hit to the region of *cow corner*, or thereabouts, as a ball landing in that area of the field will have usually come about from an unorthodox stroke. It's thought to derive from the days when aristocratic landowners would organise matches with and against their friends on their own grounds, and the local farm-workers – chosen to complete the teams – would demonstrate a considerably more gung-ho approach to batting than the refined, textbook technique of their employers.

air hostess

[cricket] – *a ball hit particularly high*

Upon seeing Sourav Ganguly safely take a difficult catch in the outfield, former Indian batsman-turned-commentator Navjot Singh Sidhu remarked that the 'ball went so high it could have got an air hostess down with it'.

albatross

[golf] – *a score of three under par on a hole*

The term *albatross* came into use by golfers in the late 1930s in the UK and later across Europe, developing from the established **birdie** and **eagle**, which had been in use since earlier in the century. Most golfers never achieve an albatross in their entire career, as indicated by the rarity of bird chosen to represent this feat. Ab Smith, American co-creator of the term 'birdie' in 1899, referred to it as a *double eagle*, the name which most American golfers still use today.

Albiceleste

[football] – *the Argentine National team*

Translated literally from Spanish as 'the white and sky blues', it of course refers to the coloured stripes on the team's shirts – a permanent feature since 1911.

All Blacks

[rugby union] – *the nickname for the New Zealand national team*

In 1905, the New Zealand rugby team made their first tour of Britain. They embarked on the tour as *The Originals* but returned as the *All Blacks*. There are two theories for this.

After one match in which they beat Hartlepool 63-0, J.A. Buttery of the *Daily Mail* referred to them as the *All Backs*, based on the ability of their forwards to play with the speed and precision of any of the backs. When they went on to their next tour match in Taunton to play Somerset County, the whole town was covered with posters welcoming the 'All Blacks', with an extra 'l' in it due to a printer's error. The *Daily Mail* picked up the incorrect name, using it again in an article announcing the team's tour schedule through

Ireland. Billy Wallace, a player on the tour, recounts that due to the article, many people turned out to catch a glimpse of the team, 'and when they saw us go past said: "Bejasus, they are as white as ourselves, as white as ourselves."'

However, the more likely and commonly held view is that the name originated from another article by Buttery, in which he referred to 'the visit of the All Blacks, so dubbed because of their sombre football garb. The only colour not black was the silver fern on the left breast and the white of their bootlaces.'

alley-oop

[basketball] – *a manoeuvre in which the ball is thrown up so that another player running towards the basket can catch it in midair and score*

Alley-oop was first used to describe what is now known as the **Hail Mary** in American football, but over time was adopted by the game of basketball. It's thought that the elaborate American football pass acquired its original name from sports journalists who thought it resembled V.T. Hamlin's 1930s comic-strip caveman, *Alley Oop*, in action.

However, perhaps a more logical explanation for its usage for the move in basketball is that it simply derives from the French *allez-oop*, the cry of 'let's go' of a circus acrobat, prior to a giant leap.

Amen Corner

[golf] – *holes 11, 12 and 13 at the Augusta National Golf Club, Georgia*

A term coined in a *Sports Illustrated* article in 1958 by journalist Herbert Warren Wind. He used it for the second half of hole 11, all of hole 12 and the first half of hole 13, and the term was his way of summing up where all the critical action had taken place in the *Masters* that year.

It was the year of the Masters that saw Arnold Palmer (see *King*) win his first Major, with the help of a ruling in the final round that incensed runner-up Ken Venturi – to such an extent that he still challenges it to this day. The tournament's official description of the events is as follows:

Saturday evening in 1958, heavy rains soaked the course. For Sunday's round, a local rule was adopted allowing a player whose ball was embedded to lift and drop it without penalty. Sunday on No. 12, Arnold Palmer hit his ball over the green and the ball embedded in the steep bank behind it. Being uncertain about the applicability of the local rule, the official on the hole and Palmer agreed that the ball should be played as it lay and that Palmer could play a second ball which he dropped. Palmer holed out for a 5 with the original ball and a 3 with the second ball. The committee was asked to decide if the local rule was applicable and if so, which score should count.

*At No. 13, still unsure of what his score was at 12, Palmer sank an 18-foot putt for **eagle** 3. When he was playing No. 15, Palmer was told his drop at 12 was proper and that his score on the hole was 3, leading to his first major victory.*

So *Amen* conveys how that *corner* of the course helped to determine the result, effectively concluding the tournament, as it does a prayer. But it's thought that Wind also chose it to suggest the seemingly miraculous way in which Palmer played those holes that day. Reputedly he took the name from an old jazz song, 'Shouting at Amen Corner'.

America's Cup

[sailing] – *the oldest active trophy in international sport, contested in the most famous and prestigious regatta in the world*

Crafted in 1848 by Garrard & Co., Sir Henry Paget, the Marquess of Anglesey bought the cup and donated it for the Royal Yacht Squadron's 1851 Annual Regatta around the Isle of Wight. In that race, on 22 August 1851, a 30-m schooner-yacht by the name of *America* won the race by twenty minutes.

Originally known by the Squadron as *The Royal Yacht Squadron Cup* or *The RYS Cup for One Hundred Sovereigns*, it subsequently became known as *The One Hundred Guinea(s) Cup* and *The Queen's Cup*, before finally becoming simply *The America's Cup* in honour of the boat that won it in its inaugural year.

It is the oldest active trophy in international sport, predating the FA Cup by two decades and the modern Olympics by 45 years, leading the sailing community to affectionately refer to it as the *Auld Mug*.

anchor

[cricket] – *an often defensive batsman who gives away few chances in their innings*

A particular batsman can often be required to drop *anchor*, steady the ship and sure-up one end when his side are entering a troublesome part of an innings as a result of a few quickly and cheaply lost wickets. Often very beneficial to a side, their stability at one end allows the more flamboyant shot-makers in the team to play their natural game. For this reason, they are known as the anchor.

Annie's room

[darts] – *a score of double one*

The phrase 'he's up in Annie's room' gained common usage during the First World War, as a dismissive answer to a question about the whereabouts of a particular soldier. It suggested the missing soldier was where he shouldn't have been – up to no good with Annie upstairs. Over time, *Annie's room* found its way into the phraseology of darts, and was applied in the same way: double one is not where a player should be. It usually means he's had plenty of throws at higher doubles before following the inevitable path to double one, and therefore should have finished the game long before ending up on the most difficult double.

Arabs

[football] – *a nickname for the fans of Dundee United FC*

This name was coined during the severe Scottish winter of 1962–63. Having already missed several games as a result of the ice and snow at Tannadice, by January 1963, United were desperate to play their Scottish Cup tie against Albion Rovers. So much so that the club hired a road-layer's tar-burner to melt the ice on the pitch. Although successful, it also removed all the grass as well. Undeterred, the club then ordered several lorry-loads of sand which they spread around the pitch before painting some lines on top. Amazingly, the referee pronounced the pitch playable, and the game got underway. United easily won the match 3-0, prompting some observers to suggest that they had taken to the sand like *Arabs*. The fans quickly adopted the name for themselves, the next few matches seeing some of them arriving at the ground wearing cobbled-together efforts at Arabian headgear.

Arkle

[cricket] – *a nickname for former Nottinghamshire and England cricketer, Derek Randall*

It was often said that Derek Randall saved at least 20 runs an innings through his prowess in the field. His hunger for the ball also often meant he could be seen actually running in from cover by the time the bowler reached the crease. He could swoop and throw in one fluid movement – and more often than not hit the *stumps*. Despite his agility and quality of throw, he was so fast that he would often run batsmen out simply by outpacing them to the wicket and whipping off the bails. His lightning run-out of Rick McCosker in the Test when England clinched the Ashes at Headingley in 1977 still amazes me when I think of it. It was this speed and agility that saw him nicknamed *Arkle*, after the legendary racehorse.

Perhaps the greatest steeplechase horse that has ever lived, Arkle was bought as an untried three-year-old for 1,150 guineas by Anne, Duchess of Westminster, in 1960. She named him after the mountain by Loch Stack in Sutherland, Scotland, that she could see from her home. He was fed two bottles of Guinness with his oats every day, perhaps contributing to his winning tally of three

consecutive Cheltenham Gold Cups; the King George VI Chase; the Irish Grand National; and two Hennessy Gold Cups. Such was his class that, when running in handicaps, he was forced to give away huge amounts of weight but nearly always romped home a winner. In his 34 races under rules, he carried at least twelve stone in 23 of them but finished with a career total of 27 victories. In many races, he would be allotted two or three stone more than his rivals, even though they were top-class horses in their own right. In the 1964 Irish National, the handicappers were forced to draw up two sets of weights – one for if Arkle ran, one if he didn't. Arkle had to shoulder at least two more stone than all his rivals. He still won.

Ashes

[cricket] – *the biennial Test Series contested by England and Australia*

This mighty cricketing clash takes its name from the 4-inch *ashes*-filled terracotta urn for which the two sides compete. The first Test match between the two countries had been played in 1877, but it was as a result of the ninth Test, and Australia's first and unexpected seven-run victory on English soil over a full-strength English side in 1882, that the young British journalist, Reginald Shirley Brooks, was inspired to write the following obituary in the *Sporting Times*:

> *In affectionate remembrance of English cricket, which died at The Oval, 29 August 1882. Deeply lamented by a large circle of sorrowing friends and acquaintances, RIP. N.B. The body will be cremated and the Ashes taken to Australia.*

Three weeks later a team led by the honourable Ivo Bligh set sail for Australia with the sole objective, as the English media put it, of 'recovering the Ashes'. Although Australia thrashed England in the first Test by nine wickets, England won the following two and so achieved their goal. This prompted a group of ladies from Melbourne to put some ashes in a small urn and present them to Bligh, saying: 'What better way than to actually present the English captain with the very object, albeit mythical, he had come to Australia to retrieve?'

For over 100 years it was believed that the urn contained the ashes of a **bail** used in the final match of the series, but in 1998 Bligh's 82-year-old daughter-in-law created considerable debate with the claim that they were the remains of her mother-in-law's veil instead. If those daughter-in-law and mother-in-law bits sounds confusing, it's because Bligh had gone on to marry one of the Melbourne women. In any case, other evidence also surfaced suggesting they were the ashes of a ball. So, although the origin of the actual Ashes is the subject of some dispute, the passion with which they are contested has never been in question.

autobus

[cycling] – *a group of riders who fall behind, but stick together to help each other finish inside the time limit for that stage*

Typically, an *autobus* – so called because of the group's slow pace and the number of people in it – will form on a mountain stage of a race. The group is composed of sprinters and flat-specialists but, most importantly, includes a *bus driver* – a cyclist with the ability to determine a pace that minimises the energy the group has to expend, but quick enough to get the autobus home within the cut-off time. If they fail to do this, they hope that by remaining in a big enough group, the officials will have to let them continue in the race – otherwise too many riders would be eliminated. This doesn't always work, however.

Otherwise known as the *gruppetto*, Italian for *little group* or *laughing group*.

back to square one

[miscellaneous] – *to start again*

Strictly speaking, this entry isn't a peculiar sporting term; it's more of a peculiar everyday term that finds its origins in sport. Nevertheless, I like it – so here it is.

On 15 January 1927, England played Wales at Twickenham. On that day, Captain Henry Blythe Thornhill 'Teddy' Wakelam, the former Harlequins rugby player, delivered the first ever live running sports commentary on the radio. With the advent of sport on the radio, the concern at the BBC was that the listener would never know where the ball was on the field. In an attempt to solve this problem, it was decided that each week the *Radio Times* would publish a grid made up of eight numbered squares that listeners could pull out and have in front of them as they listened to the commentary. Then as Wakelam identified the players and relayed what was happening, a second voice called out the number of the square the ball was in and wireless listeners around the country could follow the action on their grid. If the ball went *back to square one*, it meant that the defending side had possession of it in the very bottom left-hand corner of the pitch. And if they wanted to get themselves into an attacking position then they had to begin all over again.

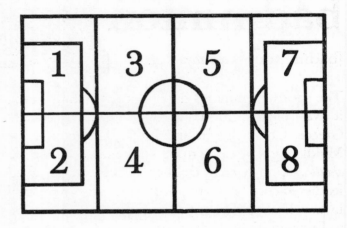

The following weekend, Captain Teddy was on duty with his microphone again, this time to watch Arsenal host Sheffield United at Highbury, and provide the first ever football commentary. To mark the 80th anniversary of that broadcast, I was recently asked to commentate on BBC Five Live for an Arsenal vs. Manchester United match for which we used the original grid commentating system. As it had died out in the 1930s, I was only mildly offended when a young producer asked me if I could remember listening to the original commentaries firsthand!

badminton

[badminton] – *a racquet sport*

The sport's beginnings date back over 2,000 years: it was played, in its original form, in ancient Greece, China, Egypt and India. Throughout the Middle Ages, it came to be known as *battledore and shuttlecock*, in which children would hit a small feathered cork back and forth with paddles covered in taut leather. The modern game was introduced to England in the 19th century by returning British army officers who developed the game while serving in India. Soon after, the sport took its name from the Duke of Beaufort's country house in South Gloucestershire, *Badminton* House, where many games were played during the 1870s. The first official rules were drawn up in 1873.

baffing spoon

[golf] – *an old equivalent to a 4-wood*

This club came from a large family of *spoons* that golfers used in the 19th century, so called because of their hollowed face. The *baffing spoon*, or *baffy* as it later became known, had a more concave face than its relatives, and was used for achieving more height over shorter distances than other spoons. It's thought that the name derives from the Old French *baffe*, meaning a blow with the back of the hand. However, the 1881 Golfer's Handbook, written by the St Andrews club manufacturer Robert Forgan, states that the baffing spoon 'is so called from the sound produced by it as it smites the ground in making the stroke'.

bagel job

[tennis] – *a set won 6-0*

American tennis player Eddie Dibbs is credited with introducing this phrase in the 1970s as a way of describing a set won to *love*, the loser's zero supposedly resembling a bagel. Being the victim of the dreaded double *bagel job*, or worse, the triple bagel job, is every player's nightmare.

Baggies

[football] – *a nickname for West Bromwich Albion FC*

West Brom settled at their current home, the Hawthorns, in 1900. They soon became known as the *Throstles*, the Black Country name for the thrush, a bird seen in large numbers in the surrounding expanse of hawthorn bushes that gave their ground its name.

In its early days, the ground only had two entrances – one behind each goal. On match days, the stewards at each gate would collect the payment from fans entering the ground and place the coins in large cloth bags. When all the fans were in the ground, the stewards would then close the gates and carry the bags of money along the touchline – escorted by police – to a small office under the stand on the halfway line. Before long it became tradition for the fans to chant 'Here come the

Baggies!' as the stewards passed the main stand. Over time, the team acquired it as their nickname as well.

During my time at Arsenal, we rarely came away from the home of the Baggies with a win and the humorous taunts from their fans live on in my memory.

baggy green

[cricket] – *the famous oversized green cap worn by Australian Test cricketers*

In 1876, when Australia played their first ever Test, every player in the team was supplied with a baggy green cap as part of a parcel of equipment. This tradition continued, with not only those on debut, but the whole team being given new caps for each tour.

Over a century later in the early 1990s, an unofficial practice emerged among Australian Test cricketers to never replace their *baggy green*. Although players can obtain a replacement cap from Cricket Australia, this very rarely occurs, with the level of wear and tear becoming an unspoken symbol of seniority among the team.

In the mid-1990s, Australian Test captain Mark Taylor introduced a prematch ceremony whereby a debutant would be presented with his baggy green by the most similar player already in the team – a tradition that has since continued under the tenure of both Steve Waugh and Ricky Ponting. On one occasion, Waugh attached further symbolism to the event by having Simon Katich receive his cap from legend Richie Benaud. 'Enjoy every single moment that you wear the cap on your head' offered one of the sport's great sages, 'and respect the traditions of Australian cricket like the many that have passed before'. In order to show solidarity among the players, Taylor also made it de rigueur for the whole team to wear their baggy green for the first session in the field of each Test match. This tradition is still strictly adhered to by everyone, Shane Warne always having to wait for the second session before he could don his trademark wide-brimmed hat.

The significance of the baggy green has been reiterated by the vast sums of money they can now change hands for, with many, even of lesser-known players, fetching anything upwards of AU$10,000 (around £4,220). In 2003, the 1953 cap of Keith Miller sold at auction for AU$35,000, with Don Bradman's 1946–47 cap selling for AU$90,000 and his 1948 cap, a phenomenal AU$425,000.

bails

[cricket] – *the crosspieces bridging the stumps*

The English adopted the word *bail* from the French in the 16th century to describe the movable horizontal part of the small *wicket* (gate) used as an entrance to a sheepfold. In early versions of cricket, this gate was often used as a target for the bowler – the equivalent of today's **stumps**, which as we know, also hold up the *bails* – the two small pieces of wood which were officially introduced to the game in 1817.

Ball of the Century

[cricket] – *the name given to Shane Warne's first-ever Ashes delivery*

In 1993, a young and unknown leg-spinner named Shane Warne made his Ashes debut at Old Trafford. In the tour matches leading up to the first Test, Australian captain Allan Border had opted to keep Warne's talents under wraps, encouraging him to bowl deliberately innocuously and allow the opposition to treat his bowling with the appropriate contempt for a newcomer.

That all changed with his first-ever ball in Ashes cricket. After a slow and short run-up, he released what appeared to be a standard leg-break to the facing right-handed Mike Gatting. Initially, it travelled straight through the air, but gradually the prodigious spin on the ball made it drift to the right, dip suddenly, and finally pitch well outside the leg stump.

Gatting had thrust his bat and pad forward and down the leg side in the normal manner adopted to defend a leg-break of this kind. As the ball had pitched outside the leg *stump* there was no danger of him being out lbw – and if the ball moved more off the pitch than expected, then the bat would be in place as defence. Needless to say, this was no normal delivery. Having drifted down the leg side, the ball bit off the pitch and moved immeasurably the other way. The deviation of the ball was far greater than normally seen on a Test pitch, especially in England, and it sailed past Gatting's pad and bat to hit his off stump. Memorably, Gatting stood and stared for several seconds in utter disbelief at the impossibility of it all before he finally accepted his fate and headed for the pavilion.

It was so utterly brilliant that the *Gatting Ball*, as it is otherwise known, was immediately labelled by the media as the *Ball of the Century* – an accolade very few have seen fit to contest.

Baltimore Chop

[baseball] – *a short downward swing intended to make the ball hit the hard ground just in front of home plate*

Executed properly, this chopping shot ensures the ball bounces high enough off the ground to give the batter sufficient time to reach first base before a fielder can catch it. Rarely used today, it was perfected by and named after the Baltimore Orioles in baseball's low-scoring early years (or the *dead ball era* as the period came to be known) over a century ago, before the emergence of big hitters such as Babe Ruth (see **Curse of the Bambino** and **Ruthian**) and the **Murderer's Row** in the 1920s. It is thought that the Baltimore groundskeeper not only packed the ground around the home plate as hard as possible, but even added clay to help increase the bounce and consequently the effectiveness of the chop. The shot itself was employed and eventually perfected by the quicker Orioles players such as John McGraw, Joe Kelley, Steve Brodie and Wee Willie Keeler.

bandy

[bandy] – *a sport played on ice with sticks, a ball and two teams of eleven players*

Bandy is sometimes referred to as *winter football*. Although an ancestor of ice hockey, it's contested on a rink the same size as a football pitch and by two teams of eleven players. Many of its rules, such as offside, are also the same as or very similar to those in football. Several English football clubs including Nottingham Forest and Sheffield United even had bandy in their original names. This is because when pitches froze over during the colder winters of the past, football teams used to keep themselves amused and fit by playing bandy instead.

It's thought that the sport takes its name from the verb *to bandy* meaning to toss hostile words back and forth.

Bantams

[football] – *the nickname for Bradford City AFC*

Bradford City is the only professional football club in England to play in claret and amber. The side inherited the colours from Manningham FC, the rugby league club which converted to association football and became Bradford City in 1903. The nickname originated as a result of some people insisting their colours resembled the plumage of the bantam. The club liked the association with the small but fearless fighting creature and so encouraged it by deliberately designing the shirt in the early 20th century so that the broad amber yolk in the middle of the claret looked like the neck and chest of the bird, ensuring the moniker stuck.

The club's scarves have sold in large numbers in recent years to fans of Harry Potter because – other than the team's badge and the Bantams nickname being at each end – the claret and amber knitted scarves are exactly the same as those worn by pupils of Hogwarts School in the books and movies.

Barbarians

[rugby union] – *an international invitational* rugby *club but with no ground or clubhouse*

The *Barbarian Football Club* was the brainchild of William Percy Carpmael from Blackheath, London. Its intended purpose was to bring together players from across the world to spread good fellowship throughout the game, and the team continues to this day. Carpmael formed the idea for the club while on tour to the north of England in 1890, late one evening over an oyster supper in Leuchters restaurant, at the Alexandra Hotel in Bradford – but the later choice of name remains a mystery. Some believe that it was named by a classics scholar who thought it 'dignified by the famous victory of Arminius over Varius and his legions in Germany some two thousand years ago', but past president of the club, Emile de Lissa, thought *Barbarian* was more likely chosen 'in defiance of those who would style all rugby players as just that'.

basketball

[basketball] – *a sport played on a hard-surfaced court with a ball and a bottomless basket at each end*

In December 1891, Canadian James Naismith, a physical education teacher at the YMCA college in Springfield, Massachusetts, USA, sought to invent a vigorous indoor game to keep his students fit during the long New England winters between the baseball and American football seasons. He drew up some rules and nailed a couple of peach baskets to the gym wall. One of his pupils called it *basketball* and the name has been unchanged ever since.

Battle of Berne

[football] – *the 1954 World Cup quarter-final between Hungary and Brazil*

On 27 June 1954, Hungary met Brazil for the World Cup quarter final at the Wankdorf Stadium in the Swiss capital, *Berne*. Pitting the beautiful flamboyance of Brazil against the free-flowing football of the **Magical Magyars** should have produced a classic. Instead it produced 42 free kicks, two penalties, several mass brawls and enough cards to ultimately see three players sent off, two of whom had to be escorted from the pitch by police.

In spite of the chaos, it's widely regarded that only the magisterial refereeing of the charming Englishman Arthur Ellis prevented the game from having to be abandoned. This view wasn't shared by the Brazilian FA however, who later lodged a formal complaint to FIFA that Ellis was part of a Communist plot devised to ensure Hungary won.

At the end of the game, which Hungary eventually won 4-2, the incensed Brazilians turned off the lights in the players' tunnel and waited for the victorious Hungarians to return from the pitch. Upon their arrival, another brawl got under way in which fists, bottles and boots flew in the darkness. As the dust settled, among a list of other injuries, it became apparent that Hungarian coach Gustáv Sebes needed stitches after being struck by a broken bottle in his face. 'This was a battle; a brutal, savage match', Sebes later said. He was right, the World Cup had never seen anything like it and the British press immediately dubbed it the *Battle of Berne*.

beamer

[cricket] – *a fast and dangerous full-toss delivery that reaches the batsman at head height*

Reputedly this delivery, when bowled deliberately, was invented by a fast bowler at Cambridge University because of his frustration at the slow and innocuous pitch at Fenners, the team's home ground. Achieving little success, he decided to upset the batsmen by bowling at their heads. Long before sightscreens were introduced, Fenners was notorious for the difficulty batsmen faced in detecting the flight of the ball due to the dark background of trees.

The obvious suggestion for this delivery's name is as a derivation of *beam*, meaning something straight and direct. However, it might possibly have been borrowed from the biblical phrase *a beam in one's eye*, which indicates that you are more at fault than those with only a splinter in theirs.

bean ball

[baseball] – *a pitch aimed at the head of the batter*

In the game of cricket, a **beamer** is also sometimes referred to – especially in Australia – as a *bean ball*. This is based on the ball being delivered at the bean, an old-fashioned colloquialism for the word *head*. In cricket, the bowler is generally given the benefit of the doubt that it is an unintentional mistake on their part and that the ball has slipped from his or her hand prematurely upon delivery. However, in baseball, a bean ball is more sinister as it is used to refer to a pitch where the sole intention is hitting the batter. As a result, a pitcher with a reputation for *beaning* is known as a *headhunter*.

On 16 August 1920, Cleveland Indians shortstop Ray Chapman was *beaned* by Yankees pitcher Carl Mays and died in a New York City hospital twelve hours later. Although Chapman is the only player to have been killed in the history of Major League Baseball by a bean ball, the pitch has cut short the careers of a number of players over the years, notably Mickey Cochrane, Tony Conigliaro and Dickie Thon. It is therefore taken very seriously and often leads to the batter charging the mound and the entire batting team climbing out of their dugout for a mass brawl with the fielding side.

Becher's Brook

[horse racing] – *a fence at Aintree Racecourse, near Liverpool, Merseyside*

Probably the most famous fence in sport and one I used to stand beside when previewing the Grand National for the BBC. Although only a modest 4'10" high on the side of take-off, the problems lie with a further two-foot drop on the other side. The drop used to be much more severe on the inside of the track but was levelled off in 1990 following the deaths of Brown Trix and Seeandem in the 1989 Grand National.

The fence takes its name from one Captain Martin Becher. Riding in the first ever National in 1839, his mount Conrad ploughed into the fence depositing the Captain in the brook on the other side. For the sake of his safety he had to remain in the water while the rest of the field thundered overhead. Upon emerging from the brook he is reputed to have said to a steward that he had not known 'how dreadful water tastes without the benefit of whisky'. He decided never to compete in the National again.

bed & breakfast

[darts] – *a score of 26*

A relatively common total from three darts as a result of hitting 20, 5 and 1 when aiming for treble 20. It's also known as the *two and six*, from which it derives its name: two shillings and sixpence was the traditional cost of a night's lodging early in the 20th century.

The term is often abbreviated to simply *breakfast*. If you get a treble 20, treble 5 and treble 1 in the same throw, then you've got yourself a *champagne breakfast*.

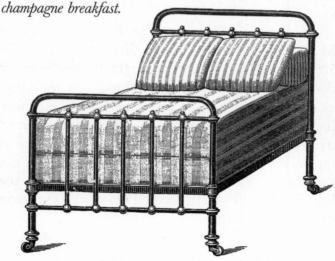

Bhoys

[football] – *a nickname for Celtic FC*

Soon after the club was founded in 1887, the team acquired the popular moniker of *Bold Boys* from its fans. It's thought by the club that a postcard from around the end of the 19th century – which referred to the Celtic team as the *Bould Bhoys* – is the first tangible evidence of this peculiar spelling. Reputedly, the additional *u* in *bold* and *h* in *boys* was an attempt to indicate the Irish pronunciation of the phrase. The new spelling stuck, but over time it became abbreviated to simply the *Bhoys*, and the name stands to this day.

Big Easy

[golf] – *a popular nickname for professional golfer Ernie Els*

'Perhaps the epitome of the slow-motion swing is the *Big Easy*, Ernie Els. What a marvel is the power that's produced by that big, slow-motion arc', wrote Dr Tom Dorsel in a Golf *Illustrated* article in February 2001. This is not the first use of the nickname by any means, but it does help to illustrate how, along with his easygoing demeanour, the 6'3" South African gained it.

Recently the golf world has seen the emergence of young female phenomenon Michelle Wie. Comparisons have been made between the styles of Els and Wie due to her 6'0" stature and her elegant and relaxed swing. This led Tom Lehman to give her the nickname, the *Big Wiesy*.

birdie

[golf] – *a score of one under **par** on a hole*

In 19th-century American slang, the term 'bird' was used to describe anything good. Reputedly, *birdie* originated in golf in 1899, during a game between Ab Smith, his brother William Smith and George Crump at the Country Club in Atlantic City. On the par-4 second hole, Ab Smith hit his second shot to within inches of the hole and exclaimed he had hit 'a bird of a shot'. He suggested that if one of them played a hole in one under par, then that person should receive double the money from the others, and all agreed. He duly holed his putt to win with what they called, from that point on, a birdie.

Bismarck

[horse racing] – *a favourite that bookmakers do not expect to win*

This term derives from the famous Second World War German battleship, named after the 19th-century German chancellor Otto von Bismarck. After it sank the flagship and pride of the British Royal Navy, HMS *Hood*, in the Battle of the Denmark Strait on 24 May 1941, Churchill despatched every available ship with the sole intention of sinking the *Bismarck*.

The *Bismarck* was a feat of engineering for the time, with armour nearly fourteen inches thick and carrying guns with a range of 24 miles. In spite of her brawn, she was also capable of a top speed of 30 knots, making her one of the fastest ships in the world.

However, on 26 May a squadron of Swordfish torpedo bombers from the aircraft carrier *Ark Royal* launched an attack and hit her three times. Two of the bombs had little effect but one hit *Bismarck* from the rear and jammed her rudder and steering gear, rendering her pretty much a sitting duck. Overnight, four Royal Navy boats rounded on her and the following morning, just before 9 am, started an attack that lasted nearly two hours.

Despite this pummelling, she wouldn't sink. Two Navy battleships even ran out of shells and set off for home. It wasn't until HMS *Dorsetshire* launched three final torpedoes from relatively short range that she succumbed and disappeared to the bottom of the sea. However, some strongly maintain that although the battleship's upper works were almost completely destroyed, her hull was still relatively intact – and that her own crew, rather than risk her being captured, scuttled her themselves. If this was the case it's not clear who gave the order as the ship's captain was presumed dead earlier after a sixteen-inch shell hit the bridge. Some survivors however, also report that they saw him going down alive with his ship. Either way, *Bismarck*, considered unsinkable by many, had lost and was on its way to the sea floor.

Black Cats

[football] – *a nickname for Sunderland AFC*

There are various links between the club and the *black cat* stretching back over the last 200 years. In 1805, a nearby gun battery on the River Wear was renamed the Black Cat battery after a number of workers heard a mysterious wailing that turned out to be a black cat trapped inside the factory. Then there's a photograph from 1905, a hundred years later, of F.W. Taylor, the club chairman, with a black cat sitting on a football next to him – and three years later, in 1908, the black cat crept into a full team photograph.

Before long, black cats were featuring in the match day programme and in club-related cartoons in the local paper. For the FA Cup Final in 1937, many fans wore a specially made black-cat tie-pin to hold their red-and-white buttonhole in place. After the same final, the press made much of twelve-year-old Billy Morris and his black kitten, which sat in his pocket at Wembley throughout that game – supposedly bringing the team sufficient luck to come from behind and beat Preston 3-1. For years, a black cat also lived at Roker Park, where it was looked after by the club, and its arrival sparked a long winning streak.

Despite all this, it's only recently that the name was properly adopted by the club. It has had a number of nicknames in its history, including the *Roker Men* and the *Rokerites*, but the move from Roker Park in 1997 left these redundant. It's only now, fully ensconced at the Stadium of Light – with their match-day mascots Samson and Delilah – that Sunderland have truly become known as the *Black Cats*.

bodyline

[cricket] – *fast bowling aimed at the batsman's body*

Also known as *fast leg theory*, this tactic was in use for some time before England's tour of 1932–33 when it was most infamously used, and named *bodyline* by the press. Douglas Jardine, the English captain on the tour, instructed his fast bowlers to bowl directly at the bodies of Australian batsmen in the hope of them directing easy catches to a stacked and close leg-side field. Although this tactic managed to keep the brilliant Don Bradman in check and consequently won England the **Ashes**, it caused several injuries to the Australian batsmen and became a full-blown political furore. 'I've not travelled 6,000 miles to make friends. I'm here to win the Ashes', was Jardine's response.

The laws of cricket came under scrutiny and saw several changes over the following decade to prevent another *Bodyline Series*, as it came to be known.

bogey

[golf] – *a score of one more than **par** on a hole*

I always have plenty of *bogeys* on my card. The name for these little blighters originated with the character called the *Bogey Man* in a popular British song from the 1890s. Later he became known as *Colonel Bogey*, and with this the song became 'The Colonel Bogey March'. Colonel Bogey was an elusive figure that hid himself wherever and whenever he could: 'I'm the Bogey Man, catch me if you can' he teased. Initially, bogey meant the same as par, i.e. the ideal score for the hole. As a result, and as suggested by the lyric 'catch me if you can', golfers chased the Bogey Man on the course in search of the perfect score.

In the early part of the 20th century, however, the meaning of the term changed. According to other lyrics in the song, the Bogey Man was very much someone to fear, so bogey became one over par, i.e. a score to be avoided.

bolo punch

[boxing] – *a combination of a hook and an uppercut*

The key to this unconventional punch is the exaggerated and undisguised wind-up before its delivery. By making it appear obvious where the next punch is coming from, the intention is to create an element of doubt in the opponent. They're left debating whether it's a trick and if they should expect a sneaky punch from the other hand, or whether it really is a build-up to what can often be a knockout blow.

The 1930s Filipino boxer Ceferino Garcia is commonly referred to as the inventor of the punch. When asked once how he came to develop the unusual uppercut, he said that it was the same technique he used to wield a *bolo* knife while cutting sugarcane in his home country as a child. The

Ceferino GARCIA

boxing media subsequently labelled it the *bolo punch* – a term that was to stick in the 1940s, when the technique was popularised by the Cuban boxer, Kid Gavilan.

However, it appears that the first practitioner of the punch was another Filipino boxer by the name of Macario Flores. According to a copy of Washington's *Tacoma News Tribune* from 27 March 1924: 'Flores lets his right hand go just as his countrymen throw a bolo knife. The blow is not only hard, but it is as fast as a streak of lightning, being almost impossible to follow with the human eye.'

bonspiel

[curling] – *a tournament*

Bonspiels are ***curling*** tournaments that originated in Scotland on frozen freshwater lochs. Outdoor bonspiels are now a very rare sight in the country as a result of global warming. The word is an amalgamation of the French *bon*, meaning *good*, and German *spiel*, meaning *game*, and is thought to have been inherited by the Scots from the invading Vikings, who invented their own language as they rampaged across Europe.

Booming Cannon

[football] – *a nickname for Hungarian legend Ferenc Puskás*

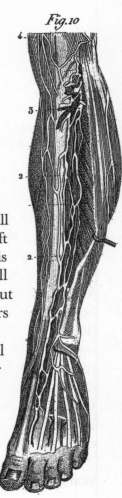

He was short, stocky, barrel-chested, overweight, couldn't head the ball and pretty much only used his left foot. Nevertheless, his left foot is perhaps the greatest the football world has ever seen and he is, without question, one of my favourite players of all time.

Born in Budapest on 2 April 1927, Ferenc Puskás began his career as a junior with Kispest Athletic Club where he played under an assumed identity – Miklós Kovács – until his twelfth birthday, when he was officially old enough to join in. He made his professional debut at the club aged sixteen. In 1949, as Communist rule spread across Eastern Europe, Kispest was taken over by the Hungarian Army and its name changed to Honvéd. As a military institution, players were assigned ranks and, in time, Puskás was appointed a major. He went on to win five Hungarian League titles with the club, scoring 357 goals in 349 games. He became known as the *Galloping Major*.

In 1956, while Honvéd was on tour in Spain, the Hungarian Revolution erupted in Budapest. When the uprising was crushed by the invading Soviet Union, many of the team, including Puskás, decided not to return. It effectively saw the break up of not only Honvéd, but the great Hungarian national side, the ***Magical Magyars***. This team had dominated world football throughout the 1950s, with the Galloping Major scoring 84 goals in 85 international appearances since his debut, aged eighteen.

Puskás was suspended from football for two years by FIFA at the behest of the Hungarian FA which branded him a traitor. In 1958, at the age of 31 and considerably overweight, he was signed by Real Madrid. In the next nine years, he played 261 matches for the Spanish giants, scoring 236 times. He was *pichichi* on four occasions, guiding the club to five consecutive La Liga titles and three European Cups. To Real fans – as an extension of his existing military nickname and because he possessed the most searing left foot they had ever seen – he became known as the *Booming Cannon*.

As far back as 1953, I remember watching him play at Wembley against England. I was utterly transfixed as he controlled the ball with his left foot, dragged it back and sent England captain Billy Wright the wrong way, 'like a fireman running to the wrong fire' as one paper said – before lashing an unstoppable shot past England keeper Gilbert Merrick. It was one of the best individual goals I have ever seen.

Boot Hill

[cricket] – *short leg*

This scary fielding position takes its name from the infamous cemetery in Dodge City, Kansas, where a large number of 19th-century American gunfighters were buried. It became known as *Boot Hill* due to the fact that most of the people laid to rest there 'died with their boots on', a euphemism for the violent and sudden way in which they met their fate.

boxing

[boxing] – *a combat sport in which two competitors trade punches with fists enclosed in leather gloves*

Although fighting with fists as a sport can be traced back to earlier than 4,000 BC, the term *boxing* did not come into use for another six millennia. Having almost entirely died out as a sport right across Europe with the fall of the Roman Empire in AD 476, it was not until 1681 that the *London Protestant Mercury* documented England's first bare-knuckle *prizefight*. In 1719, James Figg became the first heavyweight boxing champion. With the introduction of the title, came the sport's name: it was considered that the clenching of the fist with the thumb laid over the fingernails – as was the style at that time – formed a so-called *box*, and so the throwing of these fists came to be known as boxing.

brassie

[golf] – *an old equivalent to a 2-wood*

This was a wooden club with more loft than a driver but less than the *spoon* (the equivalent of the 3-wood, so called because of its slightly hollowed face). It takes its name from the fitted brass sole plate first added to the club in 1885 at Musselburgh Links, East Lothian (see **The Graves**). Members who regularly sliced their **guttie** onto the road that ran alongside the first three holes needed something to protect the underside of their club for their return shot and so added the plate. It subsequently became known as the *brassie*.

Brickyard

[motor racing] – *a nickname for the Indianapolis Motor Speedway, Indiana, USA*

Home of the legendary Indianapolis 500, host of the US **Grand Prix**, and self-proclaimed Racing Capital of the World, the Speedway's glorious history had an inauspicious start. When it opened in August 1909, the track was made simply of coarse crushed rock and tar – a surface that was to prove disastrous. Its very first race was stopped less then halfway through and, after a continued spate of horrific accidents, the track was abandoned after only a few days' use.

In the autumn of that year a new surface was built: 3.2 million paving bricks were imported by rail from the Western part of the state, laid on their sides in a bed of sand and secured with mortar. Indianapolis Motor Speedway had become the *Brickyard*.

In 1936, asphalt began to be applied to the rougher parts of the circuit, and by 1939 only 650 yards of bricks on the main straight remained. This section survived until 1961 when it too was covered over, except for three feet of bricks at the start and finish line. This symbolic strip and the Speedway's nickname have both remained as a nostalgic reminder of its glorious and chequered past.

Brockton Blockbuster

[boxing] – *a nickname for Rocky Marciano*

The first boxer I remember admiring as a young boy was Rocky Marciano. Weighing-in at a sizeable twelve pounds at his birth on 1 September 1923, Rocky was born and raised in Brockton, Massachusetts. He contracted a virulent strain of pneumonia at 18 months of age, and his doctor claimed it was only his particularly strong constitution that kept him alive. At fifteen, playing baseball for his local team, he hit a home run out of Brockton's James Edgar Playground – which reputedly landed on the front porch of a house 330 feet away. At 24, he embarked on a career as a professional boxer. After winning 37 fights by knockout, he fought Jersey Joe Walcott for the Heavyweight Championship of the World on 23 September 1953. Despite being knocked down in the first round and being behind on points for the first seven, Rocky knocked out Walcott with what's regarded as one of the most devastating punches in boxing history – a punch he thereafter referred to as his *Susie Q.*

The *Brockton Blockbuster* defended his title six times, the only world heavyweight champion to retire with a perfect record. His entire professional record of 49 fights, 49 wins and 43 knockouts may never be matched. It's not difficult to see how he acquired the name.

broom wagon

[cycling] – *a support vehicle that follows and picks up riders that retire in a stage race*

Introduced at the Tour de France after mountain stages were added in 1910, the vehicle acquired the name based on its task of 'sweeping-up' exhausted riders who fall too far behind in the race. It sometimes has broom bristles attached to the front bumper or a whole broom bolted to the car in a wonderful bit of symbolism that's sadly seen less and less in the modern era. Before entering the broom wagon, the rider must suffer a further humiliation as they have their dossard or back number removed from their jersey by an official. Also known as a *sag wagon.*

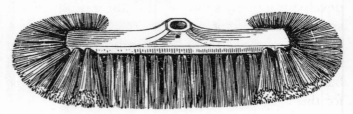

bullseye

[darts] – *the central spot of the dartboard, worth 50 points*

The term *bullseye* was first used towards the end of the 16th century as a name for the thick spherical piece of glass that was set into the deck of a wooden ship to help illuminate the gun decks below. The name gained popular usage over the following century to describe pretty much anything that was small, round or spherical. By the 18th century, with the proper advent of archery as a sport rather than simply an instrument of war, a standard target was used for which the central spot also became known as the bullseye. In time, the term was adopted by the game of darts with the development of its board and the similar, albeit smaller, central spot.

The increasing number of modern dartboards with black rather than the traditionally red bullseyes has seen the advent of the term *striking oil* for those that manage to hit it.

bumper

[cricket] – *a fast and short-pitched delivery intended to reach the batsman at chest or head height*

Because of potential danger to batsmen from this hostile delivery, the laws of cricket stipulate how frequently it may be bowled, taking into account the relative skill of the batsman. *Bumper*, based on the frequency with which the ball would *bump* into the batsman, is really a term from the past – the delivery has acquired the more self-explanatory name of *bouncer* in recent times.

Bunsen

[cricket] – *a pitch favourable to spin bowlers*

From the cockney rhyming slang *Bunsen burner*, meaning a *turner*.

Burlington Bertie

[horse racing] – *odds of 100/30*

The term *Burlington Bertie* comes from the old popular music hall song of the same name. Chosen as rhyming slang, it's sometimes also referred to as *scruffy and dirty*.

Burma Road

[golf] – *the famous West Course at Wentworth* ***Golf*** *Club*

I love playing this golf course, which has just had a makeover under the guidance of the ***Big Easy***. Originally designed by Harry Colt and opened in 1926, *Burma Road* is the most televised course in Britain, playing host to both the World Match Play and the PGA Championship every year. The ***Ryder Cup*** was also held there in 1953.

Upon the outbreak of the Second World War, the British army commandeered the club and built an elaborate network of underground bunkers, including a secret headquarters that still lies deep beneath the clubhouse. To prevent enemy aircraft landing on the fairways, the course was allowed to grow wild, but towards the end of the war this was no longer a concern. German POWs from an internment camp in nearby Egham were brought in to clear the vegetation. 'Let this be their Burma Road', one of the British officers reputedly said.

caddie

[golf] – *the person who carries a golfer's clubs and assists with choice of club, reading of greens, etc.*

Caddie comes from the French *cadet* meaning *boy* or *youngest*. Traditionally in France, the youngest sons of aristocratic families would join the army, and it's thought that these military cadets, as they came to be known, would sometimes be used to carry the clubs of Royal golfers; a practice also applied in Scotland upon the return of Queen Mary Stuart in 1561. The word 'cadet' appears in English for the first time in 1610.

In Scottish towns in the 18th century, particularly in and around Edinburgh, there were a large number of men trying to make a living as a porter or messenger, especially by delivering water. As many of these men were ex-army, they came to be known as caddies. There are many references to the carrying of golf clubs by these odd-job men of the time, but it wasn't until the following century that 'caddie' was used almost exclusively for those employed for this task.

Calamity Jane

[golf] – *Bobby Jones's famous putter*

One of the greatest golfers of the early 20th century, and indeed of all time, was Bobby Jones. His putter, with a simple offset blade, was made in 1900 – and was already twenty years old and nicknamed *Calamity Jane* when it was given to Jones in 1920. Jones replaced it in 1926 with a putter made by Spalding, which he called *Calamity Jane II.* He won ten more major championships and retired in 1930 – winning the **Grand Slam** (all four majors in one year, though these are not the same four majors as today's Grand Slam). Jones became a consultant to Spalding, which made many Calamity Jane models between 1932 and 1973. Jones gave Calamity Jane II to the USGA Museum, while the original is held by Augusta National **Golf** Club.

Calcutta Cup

[rugby union] – *a trophy for which England and Scotland have competed since 1879*

In Calcutta on Christmas Day 1872, two teams of twenty men each, one representing England and the other Scotland, Ireland and Wales, played the first game of rugby football India had ever seen. It was a resounding success and they repeated the fixture the following week. Despite the unsuitable Indian climate, a group of them wanted to establish the game in the country and so, in 1873, formed the Calcutta Rugby Club. It thrived in its first year but gradually members turned to polo and tennis due to, among other things, their greater suitability to the local climate. A number of members also left when they stopped the free bar at the club!

In time, the remaining members decided to disband, but were determined to keep the club alive in some form or other. They withdrew the club's remaining funds from the bank and had them melted down and made into a trophy which they

presented to the Rugby Football Union (RFU) in 1878, on the condition that it be competed for annually. The RFU obliged, deciding it should be contested for by England and Scotland. The first *Calcutta Cup* match, played on 10 March 1879 at Raeburn Place in Edinburgh, ended in a draw. England became the first winners of the trophy when they played on 28 February the following year.

The trophy is still contested to this day, now as part of the Six Nations Championship. In 2004, the governing bodies of rugby in both England and Scotland considered adding an additional Calcutta Cup fixture to the calendar, outside of the Six Nations. They proposed that one nation would have to win both matches to take the trophy from its current holder, but the idea was met with a largely unfavourable reaction and so was dropped.

can of corn

[baseball] – *an easy catch for a fielder*

It's thought that this term originated towards the end of the 19th century, deriving from the traditional habit of American groceries at that time to stack canned goods high against the wall behind the counter. A sales clerk would then use a wooden stick to knock the cans individually from the top of the display when needed, before catching them easily with an open hand or outstretched apron.

Canaries

[football] – *the nickname for Norwich City FC*

Norwich City FC was formed by a group of friends in 1902. Their song, 'On the ball, City', is thought to be the world's oldest football song still in use today. Originally the team was nicknamed the *Citizens* and played in blue and white halved shirts with white shorts.

Canary-breeding was a pastime practised by a large number of people in Norfolk at that time, including one of the early managers at the club who often referred to his players as his *Canaries*. By the summer of 1907, the name had gained sufficient popularity that the team began to wear yellow shirts.

With crowds continuing to grow and the landlords of the team's ground placing unworkable terms in a proposed new lease, a new venue was required. And so, in 1908, they moved to *Ruymp's Hole*, a disused ancient chalk pit in

Rosary Road. The stands from their previous home at Newmarket Road were ferried across the city by horse and cart and built precariously into the steep quarry sides, resulting in a football ground unlike any other. It became known as the *Nest*, and it was there that the name Canaries well and truly stuck.

cap

[football] – *an appearance for a national team*

This term can be used for any sport but, because of its origin, is most closely linked to football. On 10 May 1886, a new concept was approved in the United Kingdom whereby each and every player representing their country would receive a commemorative piece of headgear for an international match. The practice came about as a result of the proposal by the Old Corinthian player N.L. Jackson: 'That all players taking part for England in future international matches be presented with a white silk *cap* with a red rose on the front, these to be termed "International Caps".'

Uniquely, I have England caps (England Schoolboys 1957) and Scottish caps (Full Scottish International 1971–2), and these are among my most prized sporting possessions.

carpet

[horse racing] – *odds of 3/1*

This term derives from criminal slang for a three-month stretch in prison. 33/1 is known as a *double carpet.*

carreau

[boules] – *throwing and landing your ball directly on top of the winning ball of the opposition, not only knocking theirs away, but also leaving yours in the exact position vacated by the other ball*

This is the most difficult shot in boules – but should you master it, you have a chance in any match. Many players are good at this at home, but the precision required is such that, due to unfamiliar surroundings and additional pressure, it's a much rarer sight in competition. Its name is thought to derive from the fighting term *rester carreau* meaning *to remain on the spot* or *to be laid out cold.*

catch a crab

[rowing] – *to sink the oar too deeply into the water, causing the boat to jolt violently*

This unpleasant moment for a rower is called to *catch a crab* as it feels like a crab has grabbed the blade of the oar under the water. In the worst cases, rowers are thrown from the boat or the boat is even flipped. The first use of the term is unknown.

catgut

[tennis] – *a strong cord used for stringing racquets*

Natural gut has been used for sports racquet strings for centuries – taken from a number of animals but never from a cat. So why is it called *catgut*, when the thought of using moggy's intestines to produce searing cross-court winners continues to horrify cat lovers across the world?

In the Middle Ages, Welsh troubadours played a type of fiddle that supposedly sounded like a cat meowing. The English, not particularly impressed with the instrument, referred to it as the *cat*, and to the strings making the peculiar noise as catgut. By the 14th century, when natural gut was also used to string the very first sports racquets, the name had already stuck.

cats on the counter

[darts] – *to win a game*

 During the 19th century, *cat* and *kittens* were recognised sizes of pewter drinking pots in public houses. Upon winning a game, it was customary of the victors to point out to their defeated opponents that it was their turn to get some *cats* – the larger quart-sized pots – lined-up on the bar, or *counter*, before the following game.

chequered flag

[motor racing] – *a black-and-white flag waved at cars as they cross the finish line to signal the end of the race*

The true origin of the chequered flag seems to be lost in time but several theories abound. Some believe that it originated with horse racing during the early days of the settlement of the American Midwest; the racing would be followed by large public meals and to signal that the food was ready and that the racing should come to an end, the women would wave a large chequered tablecloth. Others think that it evolved from the early days of the Tour de France when stewards wore black-and-white chequered vests to indicate to cyclists which way to go. In time, the chequered material was placed on flagpoles instead, including one at the end of each stage. However, probably the most likely – but unfortunately least interesting – theory, is that it was chosen simply because it was easily seen against the multi-coloured background of spectators and buildings in early races.

chin music

[cricket] – *continued fast and short-pitched bowling*

Originally a euphemism for punching someone in the jaw dating back to 19th-century America, it was adopted by the cricketing world in the 1980s to describe the attack of the fast West Indian bowlers of the time. With the likes of Joel Garner and Malcolm Marshall bowling continuously short on the lively Caribbean pitches, the ball flying at 95 mph past the trembling chins of English batsmen was a common sight.

Chinaman

[cricket] – *a ball from an orthodox left-arm wrist-spinner, which turns the opposite way to the normal delivery from this type of bowler (i.e. left to right instead of the usual right to left)*

This term is thought to come from the series between England and the West Indies in 1933. At the Old Trafford Test, Ellis Achong, the West Indian left-arm spinner of Chinese descent, had English batsman Walter Robins stumped by several yards. Reputedly, on returning to the pavilion, Robins exclaimed to the umpire, Joe Hardstaff Snr., 'Fancy being done by a bloody *Chinaman*!', and that's where it started.

Chipolopolo

[football] – *the nickname for the Zambian national team*

Chipolopolo means *the Copper Bullets*. The moniker was chosen as copper is the south-central African nation's main export and bullet to suggest the speed, accuracy and deadly instincts of their players – qualities that took the side to the final of the African Nations Cup in 1994, despite losing eighteen members of their squad and their national coach in a plane crash on their way to a World Cup qualifier in Senegal, only months before. Although they narrowly missed-out in the final, losing 2–1 to Nigeria, the newly rebuilt side became national legends.

choke

[golf] – *to crack under the pressure and lose from a seemingly winning position at the climax of a tournament*

Although this can of course occur in any sport, it's perhaps most easily detected within professional stroke-play golf. Arguably its most severe example came at the **Masters** at Augusta in 1996. In the opening round, Australian Greg Norman carded a course-record 63. Three days later he managed to go round the same eighteen holes in fifteen strokes more. His brilliance over the first three rounds had seen him start the final day with a six-stroke lead – the biggest in Masters' history – over Nick Faldo, his nearest rival. He looked set to take home his first **Green Jacket**. However, by the back nine, Norman had surrendered his lead, and by the 18th green, the tearful Australian had fallen a further five shots behind the victorious Faldo, in one of the most dramatic collapses in Major Championship golf.

Although only gaining widespread usage in the 1960s, the term is thought to have originated with the Salem witch trials in the 17th century. Women were made to eat a Holy Communion wafer, the rationale being that a witch would find it impossible to swallow. Although a relatively simple task, with their life at stake, a large number of women were found guilty and executed as a result of *choking* under the pressure.

Claret Jug

[golf] – *a popular name for the trophy contested annually at the Open Championship*

This is one of the most prized and stylish trophies in sport. Despite its official name of the *Golf Champion Trophy*, the prize acquired the more widely used *Claret Jug*, as that's exactly what it is. Created in 1873 by Mackay Cunningham & Co. of Edinburgh, thanks to a contribution of £10 each from Prestwick, the Royal and Ancient Golf Club of St Andrews, and the Honourable Company of Edinburgh Golfers, it was commissioned and made in the style of elaborate silver jugs used at the time to serve red wine from the famous region of Bordeaux.

Clockwork Orange

[football] – *a nickname for the Dutch national team in the 1970s*

Although the Dutch national flag of red, white and blue is the oldest tricolour still in use today, the country's national football team play in bright orange. This comes from the coat of arms of William I of Orange – or *Father of the Fatherland* as he is known in the Netherlands – the main leader of the Dutch revolt against the Spanish in the 16th century.

From nowhere, the 1970s saw the emergence of Holland as a true footballing superpower, reaching consecutive World Cup finals in 1974 and 1978. This was largely due to their perfection of **Total Football**, or *totaalvoetbal*, a system pioneered by legendary coach Rinus Michels. In this system, if a player moves out of position, their role is immediately filled by a team-mate leaving the team formation intact. Holland became so proficient in using total football that the side became known as the *Clockwork Orange*.

I had the pleasure of playing against the brilliant Johann **Cruyff**-inspired Orange in 1971 in my second international appearance for Scotland. We managed to hold them to 1-1 in Amsterdam's Olympic Stadium until Ajax's Barry Hulshoff scored their winner in the very last minute!

cocked hat

[snooker] – *a shot in which the ball hit by the white rebounds off three different cushions towards a middle pocket*

This shot acquired its name based on the trajectory of the shot that, seen from above, resembles an old-fashioned, three-cornered *cocked hat* – a piece of formal headgear worn by particular military, naval and civilian officials from the mid-19th century until the beginning of the Second World War.

cockpit

[motor racing] – *the confined space in which the driver sits to control the car*

The first reference to this term dates back to 1587, when it was used to describe the pit dug to house cockfights. Over the following century, the term was applied to unpleasant places of combat on a more general level. Simultaneously – helped on its way by William Shakespeare, who in *Henry V* used the term to refer to the area around the stage with the lowest level of seating – it began to be used as a general term for sunken or confined spaces. For example, on British Naval vessels in the 17th and 18th centuries, the small, cramped area below deck – used as quarters for junior officers and for treating the wounded during battle – acquired the name, as did the area towards the stern of boats that houses the rudder controls. In this way, the meaning of *cockpit* developed to include any confined space used for control purposes. The term was taken up by pilots during the First World War, before finally being adopted by motor racing in the mid-1930s.

condor

[golf] – *a score of four under **par** on a hole*

Otherwise known as a *double-**albatross*** or *triple-**eagle***, this incredibly rare event takes its name from the *condor* – the largest flying landbird in the Western hemisphere. This New World species of vulture is virtually extinct, and is equally rare in the golfing world: the condor has been achieved on only three known occasions.

On 15 November 1962, at Hope Country Club in Arkansas, USA, American Larry Bruce took his drive over a cluster of pine trees on the 480-yard sharp-right dogleg par-5 5th hole. By cutting out the dogleg and clearing the trees he reached the green in one, the ball miraculously disappearing into the hole. Bruce died in 2001 but still remains a local legend.

On 24 July 1995, at Teign Valley Golf Club in Christow, England, Irishman Shaun Lynch also successfully took on a sharp dogleg 496-yard par-5 by hitting a 3-iron left off the tee over a 25-foot hedge. It went in, he went on to shoot an 88, bought drinks for all and sundry, and was subsequently given lifelong honorary membership of the club.

There's only one condor to have ever occurred on a straight par-5. On 4 July 2002, at the Green Valley Ranch Golf Club in Denver, Colorado, American Michael J. Crean hit a driver off the tee of the 517-yard 9th hole. A combination of incline, hard ground, thin air (Denver is a mile above sea level) and tail wind of 30 miles per hour saw the ball travel the unbelievable distance and go in the hole. It's the longest hole-in-one ever recorded.

corridor of uncertainty

[cricket] – *a line of delivery just outside off-***stump** *that leaves the batsman uncertain which shot to play*

Former Yorkshire and England batsman Geoffrey Boycott invented this term while commentating on the England tour of the Caribbean in 1990. 'It was a phrase I came up with on the spot', he said, and it's since been adopted by football commentators for the area between the defenders and the goalkeeper when a cross is delivered into the penalty box. In this instance, the *uncertainty* refers to the potential confusion between the players as to who will go for the ball. I hated having to try to deal with a ball delivered in this way. Fumbles by the keeper or own goals by defenders are common when the ball is delivered into the *corridor of uncertainty*.

Cottagers

[football] – *a nickname for Fulham FC*

In 1780, William Craven built a cottage where the centre circle of the Fulham pitch currently resides. The cottage was surrounded by woodland which made up part of Anne Boleyn's hunting grounds. It was lived in by a number of people for the next century until destroyed by fire in 1888. Following the fire, the site was abandoned.

Fifteen years later, it was discovered by representatives from Fulham FC who were looking for a site on which to establish a permanent home for the club. The land was so overgrown that it took nearly two years to make it suitable for football. The pitch saw its first match in 1896 and the team's new home was named Craven Cottage.

In 1905, the club called in Glasgow-born engineer and factory architect Archibald Leitch to construct a stadium. He built what's known today as the Johnny Haynes Stand, a listed building that remains one of the finest examples of football architecture, making the ground one of the most picturesque settings in league football today. However, Leitch forgot to accommodate some changing rooms in his final plans and so built the famous cottage that still stands in the corner of the ground today. Nevertheless it cemented the ground's name as Craven Cottage, and over time the team became known as the *Cottagers*.

My abiding memory of playing at the Cottage should be of proudly facing the likes of Johnny Haynes and England World Cup hero George Cohen. Instead, it's of dislocating my elbow in the first ten minutes of a game and managing to continue in goal for the remaining 80 minutes. We lost 1-0 to a Graham Leggat free kick.

Coupe Aéronautique Gordon Bennett

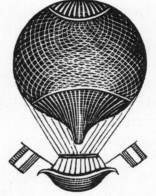

[ballooning] – *the sport's oldest and most celebrated event, the aim of which is to fly the furthest distance from the launch site*

James Gordon Bennett Jr. was publisher of the *New York Herald* in the late 19th century. He led the expensive and flamboyant lifestyle of a true playboy, indulging in yachts and lavish mansions. He was the youngest ever Commodore of the New York Yacht Club, served in the Navy during the Civil War, and in 1866, won the first transoceanic boat race.

However, he often courted controversy with his behaviour. On one occasion he arrived late and drunk to a party at the family mansion of his fiancée, socialite Caroline May, and then proceeded to urinate into the fireplace in front of his hosts and fellow guests. This would give rise to the phrase *Gordon Bennett!* as an exclamation of disbelief.

In 1906 he sponsored the *Coupe Aéronautique Gordon Bennett* which, in its inaugural race, saw sixteen balloons set off from the Tuileries Gardens in Paris, France. The winners, Americans Frank P. Lahm and his co-pilot Henry B. Hersey, landed their balloon 22 hours later in Fylingdales in North Yorkshire.

In the 1995 race, three balloons entered Belarusian air space. Despite the race organisers having informed the Belarusian government beforehand and the flight plans having been filed, the Belarusian air force shot down one of the balloons, killing the two American competitors on board. In spite of this horrendous incident, the Coupe Aéronautique Gordon Bennett still continues today.

cow corner

[cricket] – *an area of the field near the boundary between deep midwicket and long-on*

There are several theories for the birth of this cricketing term – and all somewhat unsurprisingly involve cows.

Cow corner is an unconventional fielding position and players are rarely dispatched there, leaving an area safe for cows to graze while matches are being played.

If a fielder is placed there, it's usually specifically in hopes of a catch from a high ball right on the boundary. In the early days of cricket, when pitches were in fields shared with livestock, it's thought that fielders were often too concerned with what they might be treading in to devote their attention to the ball and take the catch.

However, the most likely source of this term is the First XI pitch at Dulwich College where, in the past, there was a corner of a field containing cattle that met that part of the boundary. Captains would dispatch their fielders to what became cow corner.

coxswain

[rowing] – *the only person in the boat who doesn't actually row but is in charge of steering and giving instructions to the rest of the crew instead*

Originally a *coxswain* or *cockswain* was the boy servant or swain in charge of the small *cockleboat* or *cock* that was kept aboard the main ship and used to ferry the captain to and from the shore. The first reference to this dates back to 1463. Over the centuries, it became used for the helmsman of any boat, whatever the size, until it was adopted by the sport of rowing. The abbreviation of *cox* – as is more commonly used today – reputedly came about in the 19th century.

Crazylegs

[American football] – *a nickname for the great Elroy Hirsch*

Running back and receiver Elroy Hirsch is widely regarded as one of the best American football players of all time. He spent the majority of his professional career at the Los Angeles Rams but acquired his nickname while playing in his first college season, with the Wisconsin Badgers in 1942. In a game away to the Great Lakes Naval Training Station, Hirsch ran 61 yards for a touchdown in the third quarter. The next morning while travelling back on the train, one of his team-mates was reading the match report in the *Chicago Daily News*, which recounted the touchdown. Journalist Francis Powers had written that Hirsch 'ran like a demented duck. His crazy legs were gyrating in six different directions all at the same time.'

'Hey, Ghost, this says you have crazy legs!' his team-mate exclaimed. 'Hey, Crazylegs!' and the name remained with him for the rest of his life.

cricket

[cricket] – *a sport played with a ball, bats and wickets by two teams of eleven players*

The sport is perhaps recorded as early as the end of the 12th century, when Joseph of Exeter wrote of a game he called *cricks* being played by both men and women – although there's nothing to prove this was a form of *cricket*. Later, in the household accounts of Edward I for the year 1299, Master John de Leek, chaplain to Edward's son, was paid 100 shillings for organising the 'prince's playing at *creag* and other sports' at Newenden in Kent. Although we can't be certain that this was a type of cricket either, it does seem likely, given that this was in the heartland of cricket's history. This creag and *handyn and handoute* (another early form of cricket) gained popularity through the next few centuries, until the latter was banned by Edward IV in 1477 as he considered it a distraction from the compulsory archery practice that he imposed in order to keep his population ready for any further conflict with France.

There are no other references to the sport until 1597, when in a court proceeding over some disputed land at a school in Guildford, John

Derrick, a 59-year-old coroner, testified that 'hee and several of his fellowes did runne and play there at *creckett* … for the space of fyfty years and more'. Soon after, the name acquired the spelling that we know today. In 1611, two men from Sussex were prosecuted for playing 'cricket' instead of going to church, and in 1617, when Oliver Cromwell went to London at the age of eighteen, he was said to have 'gained himself the name of Royster' by playing 'football, cricket, cudgelling and wrestling'.

A number of words are considered to be possible sources for the name cricket. From old French there is *criquet* – meaning a type of club – that probably gave its name to the game of **croquet**, and some historians believe that the two sports have a common origin. Another theory is that the name was adopted from the Flemish *krickstoel* – meaning a long, low stool upon which one kneels in church – as a result of its profile being similar to the long, low wickets of two tree **stumps** and crosspiece used in early cricket. But probably the most likely suggestion is the Old English *cricc* or *cryce* – meaning a staff or shepherd's crook similar to the long, curved bats that were used in early forms of cricket.

Croke Park

[miscellaneous] – *the largest stadium in Ireland*

Home to the Gaelic Athletic Association, *Croke Park* in Dublin is used for Gaelic football, hurling and camogie, has a capacity of 82,300, and is the fourth largest stadium in Europe. It was named in 1913, in honour of Archbishop Thomas Croke, one of the GAA's first patrons. At that stage, it comprised a couple of stands and some grass banks. In 1917, the rubble left from the Easter Rising – a rebellion staged against British rule on Easter Monday 1916 – was used to build the famous *Hill 16* at the railway end of the pitch. Later, on 20 November 1920, as retaliation for the murder of twelve British intelligence officers earlier that day, British police auxiliaries burst into Croke Park during a Dublin–Tipperary football match, firing indiscriminately into the crowd. They killed thirteen spectators and the Tipperary captain, Michael Hogan, who has since had a stand named after him. The day became known as Bloody Sunday.

croquet

[croquet] – *an outdoor game played with a mallet and balls by two to four players*

This game is widely reckoned to have developed from a French pastime popular in the 12th century, called *jeu de mail*. By the 14th century, this had become *paille-maille* in which crude mallets were used to knock balls through hoops made of bent willow branches. By the 17th century an anglicised *pall mall* – with a curved club, a wooden ball, and two hoops – was being popularised in England by the court of Charles II. They played it in St James's Park, and the game gave its name to the nearby street that remains today.

The game lost favour during the 18th century, until it resurfaced as *crooky* in Ireland in the 1830s. Although uncertain, it's thought that the game reached Ireland via French refugees or visiting French nuns. This would corroborate the theory that the term 'croquet' is a derivation of the old French word *croche*, meaning *shepherd's crook*.

Crow's Nest

[golf] – *a room in the clubhouse of the Augusta National Golf Club, where five amateurs can stay during the **Masters***

Augusta's famous clubhouse was built in 1854 and is reputedly the first cement house ever constructed in America's Deep South. High up in the clubhouse, just below the building's famous eleven-foot-square windowed cupola, is the *Crow's Nest*. This is a single room divided into several partitions, three containing single beds; another with two beds; and a sitting area with a game table, sofa and chairs, television and telephone. There is also a bathroom and an additional sink.

Predominantly, it takes its name from being at the top of the clubhouse, a similar vantage point as a crow's nest at the top of a tree. In addition, some think the term *nest* evolved because it represents a small space in which the amateurs live before coming of age – emerging to play in the Masters, the first major of the golfing year.

Cruyff turn

[football] – *an effective move intended to lose a tracking opponent, whereby the player pretends to pass the ball but drags it back instead, turns the body and accelerates the other way*

This move takes its name from the brilliant three-time European Footballer of the Year, Dutchman Johann Cruyff. He first used it against a bemused Swedish defender during the 1974 World Cup. This was one of the nine World Cup tournaments I worked on during my TV career. I knew Johann and had played against him several times for club and country. I still rank him alongside Pelé, Maradona and George Best as the best footballers ever. When he produced this moment of magic, he took our breath away and instantly inspired a new generation of players to replicate it and add to their own skills repertoire.

curling

[curling] – *a sport played on ice with granite stones*

It's a common misconception that the name of this sport comes from the slight and deliberate spin placed on the stone as it's released, causing it to deviate (or curl) from its original straight-line trajectory. In the sport's early years, stones were simply taken from a nearby river, and their natural shape was such that the player had little or no control over them. The word *curling* first appeared in print in a poem by Henry Adamson in Perth, Scotland, in 1620. It derives from the Old English verb *to curr* which means *to growl* – a reference to the noise made by the stones as they slide across the ice. Consequently, the sport was referred to as the *roaring game* – and in Scotland, some still use this name.

Curse of the Bambino

[baseball] – *the reason cited for the failure of the Boston Red Sox to win the World Series in the 84-year period from 1920 until 2004*

In 1914, a teacher at St Mary's School in Baltimore, USA, brought George Herman Ruth Jr. to the attention of Jack Dunn, the owner of the Orioles baseball team. Upon seeing Ruth pitch, Dunn immediately signed him up to the team. Some of the older players in the side began referring to him as 'Jack's newest babe'. Babe Ruth moved to the Boston Red Sox later that year and in time would also become known as the *Bambino*, the Italian for *babe*.

Six years at the Red Sox saw Ruth become their star player, helping them to World Series titles in 1915, 1916 and 1918. A couple of years later, Red Sox owner Harry Frazee decided to sell the Bambino to the New York Yankees (who had never won a championship) to raise money for the production of his girlfriend's musical *No, No, Nanette*. Over the next 84 years, the Yankees won 26 World Series titles while the Red Sox won none, often losing to the Yankees in the most peculiar and heart-breaking circumstances. As the years passed, people began to ascribe Boston's continuing failure to the *Curse of the Bambino*.

The curse was finally lifted in 2004 when the Red Sox won the World Series (weirdly with a total lunar eclipse presiding over the ballpark – the first during any World Series game) after making an unprecedented comeback to defeat the Yankees in the American League Championship. The following year, the contract that saw the Bambino move from Boston to New York, sold at Sotheby's for US$996,000.

Curse of the Rainbow Jersey

[cycling] – *a term used to describe the terrible luck bestowed upon those that wear the distinctive jersey of the reigning world champion in a particular racing event*

In 1965, Britain's Tommy Simpson won the world title and the prospect of a lucrative following season wearing the rainbow jersey lay ahead. That winter he broke his leg while skiing.

In 1970 Belgian Jean-Pierre Monseré became the youngest cycling World Champion of all time. He was killed the following year when hit by a car during a race.

On 24 September 2006, Italian Paolo Bettini was crowned World Champion. Eight days later, his brother, who was organising a celebration of the capture of the rainbow jersey, died in a car crash, metres from his home.

In November 2006, while wearing the rainbow jersey of World *Madison* Champion, Spain's Isaac Gálvez collided with another competitor during a race and subsequently hit a railing. He died on the way to hospital.

These incidents and the numerous others have ensured that even some of the most cynical have begun to believe in the *Curse of the Rainbow Jersey*.

Dead Man's hole

[fives] – *the small three-sided niche formed where the buttress on the left-hand side of the court meets the step that separates the front and back areas of an Eton Fives court*

In medieval England, it was reasonably common for peasants to play handball against the walls of their local church. By the 17th century the game had become known as *Fives*. Although the origin of the name is uncertain, it is likely that it is based on the number of fingers on the hand used to propel the ball against the wall.

During the 19th century a number of English public schools took up the sport with their own variants. Eton Fives was born on a fairly complicated three-sided court formed by the outside wall and buttresses at the base of the school chapel steps. Although most of today's Eton Fives courts – which can be found right across the world – vary in dimension, they all must be based on the design of the court created by the chapel. This includes *Dead Man's hole*, an area based on one of the rainwater drains, so-called because if the ball lands there, it is almost impossible to return.

Derby

[horse racing] – *a one-mile, four-**furlong** and ten-yard flat race held annually on the first Saturday in June at Epsom Downs racetrack in Surrey, England*

One day in the late 1770s, while staying in a house opposite Epsom Downs, Sir Charles Bunbury and Edward Smith-Stanley (the twelfth Earl of Derby) decided that the unusual contours and beauty of the landscape would make a perfect location to race their three-year-old fillies. So, in 1779, they organised the inaugural race of this category, calling it the *Oaks* after the Earl's nearby Epsom estate.

The following year they introduced another race in which both three-year-old fillies and colts were allowed to race; the idea being that by maintaining the age limit but having horses of both sexes enter, they would be able to establish the best horse of each generation. They flipped a coin to see whom the race would be named after. Needless to say, the Earl won, and so the most prestigious flat race for thoroughbred horses in the world today became the *Derby*.

deuce

[tennis] – *the score of 40-40*

This comes from the French *à deux de jeu*, indicating that there are two points to play before the game can be won by either player. Initially, the English used the old French spelling and abbreviated it to *à deus*, before modifying it to one syllable: the more easily said *deuce*.

devil's number

[cricket] – *the score of 87, considered unlucky by Australian cricketers*

The Australian equivalent of England's *Nelson*, the *devil's number* is believed to be bad luck as it's 13 runs short of a century. Also, up until 2005, Australia had not lost the Ashes since 1987, so some think that this date played a part. The origin of the superstition is unknown.

Devil's Own

[darts] – *a score of 88*

This term takes its name from the 88th division of the Connaught Rangers, a regiment of the British Army raised in 1793 from the men of Connaught in Ireland by John Thomas de Burgh, 13th Earl of Clanricard. After distinguished service in the Peninsular, Crimean, Boer and First World Wars, the regiment was disbanded in 1922 following the foundation of the Irish Free State.

During the Peninsular War at the beginning of the 19th century, the 88th had served under Lieutenant-General Sir Thomas Picton, who ultimately became the most senior officer to die at Waterloo. Picton had been scathing of them at first, referring to them as the *Connaught Footpads* in reference to their reputation for plundering. It wasn't long, however, before he learned to appreciate their abilities when it came to a hard fight. There's much evidence to suggest that in moments of crisis in battle on the Iberian Peninsula, Picton would specifically send in the 88th to try and secure that part of the front line. Their repeated success and the manner in which it was achieved saw Picton name them the *Devil's Own*.

Doctor

[cricket] – *the nickname for the cricketing legend W.G. Grace*

Although he made considerably more money from cricket than all his fellow professional players, William Gilbert Grace was officially an amateur player. He was a medical man by profession – on one occasion having to ply his trade on an unfortunate fielder who impaled himself on Old Trafford's boundary fence – hence his nickname the *Doctor*.

Due to the inordinate time he devoted to cricket, however, it was perhaps one of the longest medical trainings in history. Beginning his study as a 19-year-old bachelor, he passed his finals as a father of three in his thirties. He came from a predominantly medical family, who similarly put cricket first – on one occasion his coroner brother put a corpse on ice just so he could attend to it at the close of play.

Doggett's Coat and Badge

[rowing] – *the prize and name of the oldest rowing race in the world*

At the beginning of the 18th century there were more than 10,000 watermen licensed to work on the Thames above London Bridge, ferrying passengers along and across the river before the grand era of bridge-building had begun. Thomas Doggett, an Irish actor plying his trade in London at the time, became very dependent on watermen to ferry him back and forth between his places of work and his residence in Chelsea. In 1715, Doggett fell overboard while crossing the Thames near Embankment but was rescued by a waterman. In appreciation, he organised and funded a race from the Swan pub at London Bridge to the Swan pub at Chelsea to be contested by six apprentice watermen. In honour of King George I, the inaugural race took place on 1 August 1715 to commemorate the first anniversary of his accession to the throne. Doggett provided the prize of a resplendent red coat and silver badge.

The four-mile, five-*furlong* race continued to be organised and funded by Doggett each year until his death in 1721. In his will, he left specific instructions and bequeathed money to the Worshipful Company of Fishmongers to ensure the continuation of the race. It has faithfully complied with his wishes ever since, making this the world's oldest-known sporting contest still in existence.

domestique

[cycling] – *a member of a professional cycling team, whose job is to ride solely for the benefit of the team and team leader, instead of their own glory*

These are used predominantly to dictate the pace of the *peloton* (the main group of riders) during a race, but are called upon in all eventualities. For example, should their team leader suffer a puncture, the *domestique* will wait with them until it's fixed, then cycle to the front in order to create a slipstream and allow the team leader to recover their position. In more extreme circumstances, they may be asked to sacrifice their bicycle should their leader's suffer irreparable damage. Although they do not share the fame of their team colleagues, a good domestique is highly respected within his sport. Sometimes they can achieve fame of their own, however, as Lucien Aimar proved when he supported the illustrious Jacques Anquetil on the 1966 Tour de France, but ended up winning it instead.

Despite *domestique* being the French word for *servant*, the French refer to this member of the team as *porteur d'eau* or *water carrier*.

The Don

[cricket] – *a nickname for Australian legend,*
Donald Bradman

Sir Donald George Bradman AC is, beyond any
argument, the greatest batsman who ever lived.
At the age of nineteen, he made his first-class debut
and scored 118. At 21, he made 452 not out for
New South Wales against Queensland at Sydney,
the highest score ever made in first-class cricket
across the world at that time. In the same year,
he scored 974 runs in only seven innings over
the course of the five *Ashes* Tests, the highest
individual total in any Test series the world has
ever seen. On one day of that series he scored 309,
still the most runs scored by an individual in a
single day's play. Against South Africa the following
year, he recorded the highest batting average for a
five-Test series there has ever been, with 201.50.

Bradman scored centuries at a rate better than
one every three innings. He converted very nearly
a third of them into double hundreds, his career
total of 37 first-class double centuries still the

most achieved by any batsman in the history of the game.

One phase of his career saw him score centuries in eight consecutive Tests, amassing the following scores: 270, 212, 169, 144 not out, 102 not out, 103, 187 and 234. His 270, in the third Test against England at the Melbourne Cricket Ground in 1937, is still rated by *Wisden* as the greatest Test innings of all time.

His career Test batting average of 99.94 is considered by some to be the greatest statistical performance in any major sport. The Australian Broadcasting Corporation obviously thought so, as they have since made their mailing address of every state capital, PO Box 9994, in honour of his remarkable achievement.

There are too many more records to mention. As former Australian batsman Jack Fingleton once remarked: 'You didn't bat with Bradman, you ran for him.'

The sport might well never see a player of his stature again. And that is why he became *The Don*.

doosra

[cricket] – *a ball that is the off-spinner's equivalent of a leg-spinner's googly, whereby the top-spinning delivery from the back of the bowler's hand turns away from a right-handed batsman*

This is a Hindi and Urdu word meaning the *second* or *other one*. It's a relatively new development in the game, with Pakistan's Saqlain Mushtaq its first successful practitioner in the mid-to-late 1990s. However, the legality of the *doosra* within the game has been called into question on a number of occasions since its inception, as many believe it's impossible to produce while retaining a legitimate bowling action.

dormie

[golf] – *the situation in matchplay when a player has a lead which equals the number of holes left*

Dormie derives from the French verb *dormir* meaning *to sleep*. The term was adopted based on the thought that a player can relax or even go to sleep without fear of losing the match. Although this is true, a halved match can sometimes feel more like a loss, as Mark Calcaveccia found to his cost at the **Ryder Cup** in 1991 – when *dormie-four* over Colin Montgomerie, he lost the last four holes, allowing the European to secure a vital half-point.

Dorothy

[cricket] – *a six*

More commonly used in Australia, it is rhyming slang derived from *Dorothy Dix*, the pseudonym for the hugely successful agony aunt of US journalist Elizabeth Meriwether Gilmer. By the time of Gilmer's death in 1951, Dix's column of advice on love and marriage was syndicated in newspapers around the world and had an estimated audience of 60 million readers, paving the way for any popular advice columnist plying their trade today.

dot ball

[cricket] – *a delivery off which no runs are scored and no wicket is taken*

After this kind of ball, the scorer has nothing to write in the scorebook other than a *dot*, which is used to indicate that the ball has taken place but that there was nothing significant to record (see also *join the dots*).

drop-in wicket

[cricket] – *a portable batting surface*

These became a necessity during the era of Kerry Packer's breakaway *World Series* (see ***pyjama cricket***) in the late 1970s when – operating outside the cricket establishment which had banned him use of all major grounds – non-cricketing venues had to be used to stage games.

Packer recruited John Maley from the ***Gabba*** as his senior groundsman who grew the pitches in 25-ton concrete trays in greenhouses next to the venue before having them literally dropped into place by crane shortly before use.

duck

[cricket] – *a score of zero by a batsman*

The term *making a duck's egg* originated in the 1860s to denote this unfortunate and quick outcome to a batsman's innings. It's thought to have started as a result of a spectator who, because a zero looks like a duck's egg, decided to quack at a disconsolate batsman as he returned to the pavilion. It's since been abbreviated to *duck* but has also gained a number of prefixes with varying meanings.

If a batsman is out third ball without scoring, he is out for a *bronze duck*. If he is out second ball without scoring off the first, he has the dubious pleasure of returning to the pavilion with a *silver duck*, and if he is out first ball, he has the joy of talking his team-mates through every last second of his *golden duck*.

On the basis that diamond is more rare than gold, a *diamond duck* is when an opening batsman is out the very first ball of the match. More rare still, although also referred to as a *diamond duck*, is when a batsman is run out without having faced a single delivery.

If an opening bat loses his wicket on the first ball of the innings it's a *royal duck*, and perhaps the most annoying of the lot – given that an opening batsman will have waited the entire winter to stride out to middle – is being out on the first ball of the season, otherwise known as a *platinum duck*.

Duckworth-Lewis method

[cricket] – *a mathematical system used to calculate revised target scores for the side batting second in a rain-affected one-day match*

This system takes its name from its statistician co-creators, Frank *Duckworth* and Tony *Lewis*. It was first used in 1997 and had taken over from its flawed predecessors by the 1999 World Cup. It's since been fully adopted by the International Cricket Council and is now the standard rain rule for first-class cricket across the world. Although the formula is apparently relatively simple to apply when needed, that doesn't mean I can explain how it works!

Duel in the Sun

[golf] – *the 18th hole on Turnberry's Ailsa course*

In 1977, Turnberry hosted the Open for the first time. It turned out to be a classic showdown between two of the game's giants. In blistering summer heat, Jack Nicklaus and Tom Watson matched each other in every round until the last, when Nicklaus shot a 66 to Watson's 65, finishing the Championship ten and eleven shots clear of the field respectively, with their 268 and 269 destroying the tournament record of 276. In recognition of this classic battle, the 18th has since been named the *Duel in the Sun.*

eagle

[golf] – *a score of two under **par** on a hole*

The term *eagle* began to be used by golfers in America in the 1920s as a development of the theme established by ***birdie*** earlier in the century. As the national symbol of the United States, the eagle was the obvious choice of bird, while it also represented the rarity and impressive nature of scoring two under par on a hole. It was adopted in Europe soon after and is now universally established across the golfing world.

early bath

[rugby league] – *a **red card***

Although now used by other commentators in other sports, this phrase was coined by the ebullient Yorkshireman Eddie Waring, while commentating on a rugby league match in the 1960s. Played predominantly in the North of England and often in its characteristic wet weather, rugby league encounters sometimes descend into a total mud-bath, with players becoming so covered in mud that it's impossible to identify them. With no players' names at his disposal, Waring would then spruce up the other aspects of his commentary to keep the viewers entertained. In one match, with the camera focusing on an indeterminate spherical object he was forced to admit: 'I don't know if that is his head or the ball. We'll see if it stands up.' Another afternoon saw the birth of the term *up-and-under* for a high kick, and when a player was sent off late in the game, Waring declared that he had been packed-off for an *early bath*.

Eddie was a lovely sensitive man and this side of his nature came out with his reaction at the climax of the memorable Challenge Cup in 1968. Wakefield Trinity scored a try in the last minute to narrow the score to 11-10, leaving Don Fox with the seemingly simple task of kicking a conversion from in front of the posts to secure victory. However, he slipped on the saturated pitch and missed, handing the victory to Leeds. As Fox slumped in the Wembley mud, Eddie's commentary was simple and perfect: 'Eee, poor lad.'

Eau Rouge

[motor racing] – *the famous chicane at Spa-Francorchamps circuit in Belgium*

Widely considered one of the greatest corners on any racetrack in the world, *Eau Rouge* takes its name from a small stream that crosses the track at this point for the first time.

Eddie would go

[surfing] – *a reference to legendary waterman Eddie Aikau, renowned for taking on waves from which others would shy away*

In 1968, 21-year-old Hawaiian surfing legend Eddie Aikau became the first lifeguard hired by the City and County of Honolulu to work on the North Shore, and given the impossible task of covering miles of coastline. He saved dozens of lives over the next three years, perhaps hundreds, as he hardly ever filed official rescue reports. In 1971, the roving patrol was disbanded and he was assigned permanently to the infamous Waimea Bay. Not a single life was ever lost on his watch.

On 16 March 1978, Aikau, keen to honour his Hawaiian heritage, set sail as part of a crew on a 2,500-mile journey that would follow the ancient route of migration between Hawaii and Tahiti. During the journey, their voyaging canoe, *Hokule'a*, developed a leak in one of its two hulls and later capsized in extremely stormy weather. They spent a night clinging to the overturned hull. In spite of being battered by waves and gale-force winds and not knowing how far they were from land, Aikau insisted on going for help. He tied the surfboard leash to his ankle, a portable strobe light and some oranges around his neck, and hesitantly tied a life  jacket around his waist. As he paddled away, crew members held hands and said a prayer. Some saw Aikau ditch the cumbersome life jacket a few hundred yards from the *Hokule'a*. They all watched as he and his board peeked back and forth into view as it rode up and over the huge waves. He gradually became smaller and smaller as he stroked away until eventually he vanished from sight.

Although the *Hokule'a* was spotted by a plane later that day and its crew saved, no one ever saw Eddie Aikau again. Nevertheless, his name would be immortalised by the term that emerged and gained widespread usage with watermen across the world after his death – *Eddie would go*.

Eel

[swimming] – *the nickname for Eric Moussambani*

Equatorial Guinea's Eric Moussambani was invited to compete in the 100-metre freestyle at the 2000 Sydney Olympics through a programme that allows a handful of athletes to compete even though they don't meet qualifying standards – an initiative introduced to spread sport around the world. He had taken up swimming only eight months before the Olympics, and until reaching Sydney had never seen a 50-metre pool.

In the heats he squared off against two other swimmers, but they were both disqualified for false starts. Moussambani was left to swim the heat by himself and having never swum that far before, only just managed to get to the finishing line to secure his place in the final. Craig Lord, the swimming correspondent for *The Times*, immediately wrote an article about 'Equatorial Guinea's aquatic answer to Eddie the Eagle – Eric the *Eel*'. Before long, the name had stuck.

In the final, while the eventual winner Pieter van den Hoogenband managed a world-record-breaking 47.84 seconds, Moussambani took more than twice as long. He splashed his way to the finish line to the rapturous applause of the 20,000-strong Sydney crowd, outside even the 200-metre world record time. 'The last fifteen metres were very difficult', Moussambani said.

Eisenhower Tree

[golf] – *a 65-ft, 120-year-old loblolly pine tree on hole 17 at the Augusta National Course*

This is named after former US President and club member Dwight D. *Eisenhower* who, having hit his ball into it so many times, proposed at a club governors' meeting in 1956 that it should be cut down. So outraged was the club's chairman, Cliff Roberts, that he adjourned the meeting immediately, and the tree has been linked with Eisenhower ever since.

In spite of this, the club did build Eisenhower his own cabin on its grounds. It was built to Secret Service security specifications, some believed, solely to protect him from the chairman!

Eskimo roll

[canoeing] – *use of the body and paddle to right a canoe or kayak after capsizing without leaving the vessel*

Eskimos are thought to have been using kayaks for over 3,000 years and to have developed this move, which is named in their honour. They developed the roll in order to minimise time spent in the freezing waters that could kill within minutes. It was also essential that they didn't fall out of the kayak, as Eskimos are thought not to have known how to swim.

Everest of the sea

[sailing] – *a nickname for the Vendée Globe*

The Vendée Globe is a solo, non-stop round-the-world race in which assistance is absolutely forbidden. The inaugural race was in 1989–90 and it's since been held every four years. It is the only race of its kind in the world.

Entrants set off from France in November, sail down the Atlantic Ocean to the Cape of Good Hope on the coast of South Africa, then clockwise around Antarctica. Keeping Cape Leeuwin (on the south-west coast of Australia) and

Cape Horn (on the south coast of Chile) to port, competitors proceed back up to France, aiming to complete the course by February.

A significant proportion of the entrants retire each year, usually as a result of the severe conditions they encounter in the South Pacific. In 1992, in only the second edition of the race and only four days after the start, British sailor Nigel Burgess was found drowned off Cape Finisterre on the west coast of Spain. It's thought that he fell overboard.

Four years later, on 8 January 1997, Canadian Gerry Roufs was in second place when his satellite positioning beacon stopped transmitting. Despite four competitors combing the ocean he couldn't be found. Later that year on 16 July, long after the race had finished, a Panamanian cargo ship found the battered remains of Roufs's boat drifting 300 miles off the coast of Chile.

Like those that have died trying to reach the summit of the highest mountain on Earth over the years, these two men lost their lives attempting to conquer the *Everest of the sea*, the highest pinnacle in the yachting world.

fairy rock

[curling] – *the granite used to make specialist curling stones*

It is a requirement of the World **Curling** Federation that all new curling stones used at major events such as the Winter Olympics must be crafted from *fairy rock*. This is taken from *Ailsa Craig*, the uninhabited volcanic island found 11 miles off Scotland's west coast (see **Postage Stamp**). Ailsa Craig – also known as *Paddy's Milestone* as a result of its location halfway between Glasgow and Belfast – comes from the Gaelic for *fairy rock*.

falling leaf

[football] – *a long-range shot which sees the ball change direction radically in the course of its flight*

In my playing era, footballs were made of thick heavy leather, which got even heavier when it rained. They went from a to b in a straight line and that was it. At the 1970 World Cup, a combination of Mexico's thin air and the unique ability of Brazil's legendary **Garrincha** to hit across the ball produced the first dramatic swerve I had ever seen. However, these days, the modern football is much lighter and if hit hard enough moves around in the air erratically enough to give the keeper a real headache. One swerve and it's a *banana*, two and it's a *falling leaf*, mimicking the path of a leaf buffeted by the air. Probably the most famous example of this came at the Tournoi de France in 1997, when another Brazilian, Roberto Carlos, blasted a 37-yard free kick wide of the French wall. Although it seemed to be easily heading out for a goal kick, it took a devastating left swerve at the last minute and ricocheted off the inside of the post into the net. The French goalkeeper at the time, Fabien Barthez, hadn't even moved.

fevvers

[darts] – *a score of 33*

This derives from the 19th-century cockney tongue-twister: 'Thirty-three thousand feathers on a thrush's throat.' In the early 20th century, London's East End was home to the dartboard manufacturing industry. As result, a large number of public houses and working men's clubs in the area had a board. The game was rife among East Enders and much of its terminology was invented at that time. So although 33 was initially represented by the term *feathers*, in a nod to their dialect, it has been assumed that a proper cockney would have said: 'Firty-free fahsand *fevvers* on a frush's froat.'

Fiery

[cricket] – *a nickname for Yorkshire and England fast bowler, Fred Trueman*

Frederick Sewards Trueman was larger than life from the word go. Born in Stainton near Maltby, West Riding (now South Yorkshire) on 6 February 1931, he weighed in at a whopping 14 pounds 1 ounce. In 1949 he made his first-class debut for Yorkshire at the tender age of seventeen. Only four years later he made his Test debut after being granted leave from his National Service in the Royal Air Force. With his trademark scowl and mop of unruly jet-black hair, Trueman inspired a seven-wicket victory for England after India were reduced to 0-4 at the start of their second innings, with three of the batsmen dismissed by the Yorkshireman in the space of eight deliveries. In his third Test he took 8 for 31 – the best Test bowling figures by a genuinely fast bowler at the time. He became a schoolboy hero of mine as the first man in the history of the game to take 300 Test wickets. Over time, Trueman's extreme pace, ability to intimidate batsmen psychologically, and his generally aggressive approach to the game, saw him labelled simply *Fiery*, or *Fiery Fred*.

John Arlott said of him: 'The kindling could be sudden and unexpected. All that anyone knew was that suddenly he was going eagerly back to his mark; there was a belligerent spring in his run, he came over like a storm-wave breaking on a beach, and followed through with so mighty a heave that the knuckles of his right hand swept the ground ... Where previously the ball had curved off the pitch calf-high, it now spat to the hips or ribs: wicket-keeper and slips moved deeper; the batsman, who had seemed established, was late on his stroke; and the whole match was transformed.'

Off the pitch, one of his favourite tricks was to go into the opposition dressing room prior to a match and say: 'Right, there's five wickets in here for me to start with.' In an *Ashes* Test in the early 1960s, as an Australian batsman emerged from the pavilion and turned to shut the boundary gate, Trueman suggested: 'Don't bother son. You'll be back soon enough.' His ability to out-psych batsmen only served to add to his considerable physical capabilities. In his prime there were only a handful of batsmen that could play Trueman with any real certainty and as a result captains would throw him the ball at every conceivable opportunity. This ensured he bowled more than 99,000 deliveries in first-class cricket. He still holds the record for the most consecutive first-class matches played in which he took a wicket (67). In spite of his massive workload he hardly missed a game through injury, his only admission of fatigue coming after he had taken his world record 300th Test wicket at the Oval in 1964. Asked whether he thought his achievement would ever be surpassed, he remarked: 'I don't know, but whoever does it will be bloody tired.'

I met Fred on a couple of occasions towards the end of his life. Both times he was friendly but characteristically blunt and I still smile when I think of our first meeting: 'Aye lad, tha's done well for thee self, except for that bad goal you let in at Cup Final!'

Upon his death on 1 July 2006, Sir John Major paid fitting tribute to the great man: 'Fred Trueman was one of the great fast bowlers of all time. He became an icon in his pomp, and remained so all his life. England has lost a national treasure and history has gained a legend.'

fish and globe

[darts] – *a score of 45*

Until the second half of the 20th century this was more commonly known as a *bag o' nuts*. The reason being, when competing on a fairground darts stall, a score of 45 would traditionally win the customer a small paper bag of peanuts. Over the following decades, however, it became more likely that a customer would be offered a goldfish in a jar or *globe*, which, in time, saw the term updated. Although some think that the term globe was chosen as a result of stall owners talking up the jar in the prize, it may be because the traditional shakeable snowglobes were becoming popular at that time and might also have been offered as a prize. Either way, if you score 45, then you've bagged yourself a *fish and globe*.

flat-track bully

[cricket] – *a specialist batsman who is only very good when batting on a benign pitch*

This term was coined by New Zealand cricketer John Bracewell back in 1989. He was referring to Graham Hick who was spending the winters of 1987–88 and 1988–89 playing in New Zealand's domestic competition for Northern Districts. Hick was enjoying great success, notching up ten centuries and averaging 63.61 in the first season and 94.46 in the second. In one game against Auckland he scored a first-class record of 173 runs between tea and the close of play!

This moniker dogged Hick throughout his career, and Bracewell's accusation would come back to haunt him in equal measure fifteen years later. Now New Zealand coach, Bracewell took his touring side to Worcestershire at the start of their summer tour. With preparations for the summer ahead very much in mind, Bracewell looked on in desperation as a 37-year-old Hick dismantled his bowling strikeforce, despatching them around the picturesque Worcester ground on his way to an unbeaten 204. As Derek Pringle succinctly put it: 'Hick made a run-a-ball double hundred against the cream of the crop on a pitch never as easy as his strokes made it appear.' You could say it was retribution complete.

flipper

[cricket] – *a faster delivery from a leg-spinner bowled with back-spin, causing it to skid off the pitch, fast and low*

This delivery was reputedly invented by the Australian Clarence Grimmett in the early part of the 20th century. He's thought to have developed and perfected it while bowling to a marked area in his backyard, using his dog to retrieve each delivery.

Once perfected, it helped him go on to become the first player to take 200 Test wickets. He bowled so many *flippers* that he prompted the great Don Bradman to suggest that he must have forgotten how to bowl his stock leg-break. In response, he bowled Bradman in a match a few days later with a leg-break.

Because of the action required by the hand to generate the flipper, it's common for the fingers to make a clicking sound as they release the ball – so in order to confuse the batsman while bowling leg-breaks, Grimmett would click the fingers on his left hand while releasing the ball from his right.

Foinavon

[horse racing] – *a fence at Aintree Racecourse, near Liverpool, Merseyside*

A fence only 4′6″ high shouldn't pose too much of a problem. Nevertheless in the 1967 Grand National it caused carnage on an unprecedented scale. On the second circuit of the world-famous ***steeplechase***, there were a few riderless horses at the front of the leading pack. When they reached the fence, the loose horses had decided they weren't going over and bolted across the track. This frightened the leaders still carrying ***jockeys*** who pulled up and refused to jump the fence. Before long there was a total pile-up with a number of jockeys being flung over the fence while their horses remained on the other side. As horses stopped ploughing into the melee and the chaos gradually untangled, none of the horses had any speed with which to jump the fence and so were forced to run the wrong way down the track so that they could come back and give it a second try.

In the meantime, a 100/1 rank outsider by the name of

Foinavon who was so far behind that he had missed the bedlam, caught up and quietly picked his way through the aftermath. He was the only horse to jump the fence at the first attempt that day and made it across with a 100-yard lead. Seventeen horses had remounted and were now in hot pursuit. Although there still a further seven fences to go, Foinavon just managed to hold on – and today, his name remains with the fence that allowed him to become the most unlikely winner the Grand National has ever seen.

football

[football] – *a sport played with a round inflated ball on a playing field with two goals by two teams of eleven players*

Man has been kicking a ball around for at least two millennia. Nevertheless, before the formation of the FA in 1863 and the subsequent introduction of a set of rules, *football* was a rowdy affair with opposing factions fighting pitched battles with the 'goals' sometimes several miles apart. Although the use of foot was the main way of propelling the ball in the mass throng of writhing bodies, the name referred to the fact that it was a game of *ball*, or *gameball*, played on foot. This helped distinguish it from the team games of the disapproving nobility, which were played on horseback.

Irrespective of the disapproving nobility of the past, I owe an awful lot to the game and one of my favourite quotes comes from the philosopher and fellow goalkeeper Albert Camus who once said: 'All that I know most surely about morality and the obligations of man I owe to football.'

fore

[golf] – a word shouted at anyone in danger of being hit by a ball

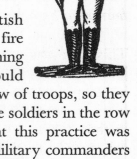

Although the definite origin of this exclamation is unknown, there are two different theories.

In the days of the British Redcoats lining up in rows to fire their muskets at the approaching enemy, the commander would shout *'Fore!'* to the 'forward' row of troops, so they kept their heads down while the soldiers in the row behind fired. It's plausible that this practice was then adapted for golf by the military commanders for whom it was a popular sport.

However, the more likely explanation comes from the practice of using two **caddies** in the 17th century; one to carry the golfer's clubs and the other, the *forecaddie*, to go on ahead to spot where the ball landed. If the player thought that the forecaddie was in danger, he would shout 'Fore!' to alert him to the approaching ball.

The standard of my golf means I use the expression a little too regularly!

Fosbury flop

[athletics] – *a method of high-jumping in which the athlete crosses the bar backwards with the body horizontal and the back facing the ground*

This technique was assigned its name by a journalist from Medford, Oregon, after being used in competition by Richard Douglas 'Dick' *Fosbury* for the first time. He started experimenting with his method through high school, before going on to win with it in 1968 at the National Collegiate Athletic Association indoor and outdoor high-jump titles while a student at Oregon State University. At the Summer Olympics in Mexico City later that year, it won him the ultimate prize – a gold medal and a new Olympic record of 2.24 metres.

Foxes

[football] – *a nickname for Leicester City FC*

Leicestershire is considered to be the birthplace of fox hunting as it is known today and the MP Hugo Meynell – who lived in the county in the 18th and early 19th centuries – is generally seen as its forefather. As a result, the symbol of the county council is the fox, a symbol that Leicester City FC adopted for its club crest in 1948, which in turn led to the nickname of the *Foxes*.

In another reference to the county's tradition of hunting, the club had adopted the *Post Horn Gallop* in 1941, the tune that the team still runs out to on home matches today.

furlong

[horse racing] – *a distance of one eighth of a mile*

For some time before the Norman Conquest in 1066, Saxon farmers in England had been using *furlongs* to measure distance. The word comes from the Old English *fuhrlang*, meaning *the length of a furrow*. It represented an eighth of a mile – theoretically, the ideal length for a field as it was the distance that a team of oxen could plough before needing a rest. Over time, this unit of distance was adopted by the horse-racing community.

futsal

[futsal] – *a form of football played indoors with a less bouncy ball and five players on each side*

Futsal was devised by Juan Carlos Ceriani in Montevideo, Uruguay, in 1930 – the same year that the country hosted the first FIFA World Cup. It soon spread to South America, particularly Brazil, where  many of the country's great footballers including Pelé, Zico, Sócrates and Ronaldinho have cut their teeth on the futsal pitch. Its name is an amalgam of the Spanish *fútbol* (football) and *sala* (room), which can be very roughly translated as indoor football.

Gabba

[cricket] – *a Test cricket ground in Brisbane, Australia*

Home of the Brisbane Lions AFL team and the Queensland Bulls national cricket team, the *Gabba* takes its name from the suburb of Woolloongabba in which the ground can be found.

Galáctico

[football] – *a world-famous and highly paid attacking player signed by Spanish La Liga club, Real Madrid*

During Real Madrid's rich and chequered history, the club and its players have acquired a number of nicknames.

Among the earliest were *Los Blancos* and *Los Merengues* with reference to the team's famous all-white strip. In the 1970s, the signing of several northern European players saw them labelled *Los Vikingos*.

In 2000, despite the club having just won its second European Cup in three years, Lorenzo Sanz lost the club presidency to former politician Florentino Pérez. Instrumental in his success was his promise to lure Portugese star Luís Figo to the Bernabéu from FC Barcelona should he be elected. On 16 July, Pérez won the coveted job. Eight days later, Luís Figo was presented with the number 10 shirt of Real Madrid. It marked the start of Pérez's policy to bring one of the best footballers in the world to the club each summer whatever the cost. At £38.7 million, the signing of Figo set a world record transfer fee. The following summer, Pérez signed Frenchman Zinedine Zidane from Juventus for £44 million – another world record.

Before long, each high-profile signing was referred to as a *galáctico* by the media in an attempt to describe these players' aura and superstar status in the world game. The following year, in 2002, the club signed Ronaldo from Inter Milan for £26 million, David Beckham for £25 million in 2003, Michael Owen in 2004 and Robinho the year after that. Collectively they had become *Los Galácticos*.

Garrincha

[football] – *the legendary
Brazilian player*

Manuel Francisco
dos Santos was born on
28 October 1933 with a
deformed spine, his right leg
bent inwards and his left leg
six centimetres shorter than the
other. His sister Rosa pointed
out that he was as small and defence-
less as a little wren, a *garrincha*.
Nevertheless, the diminutive Brazilian
went on to win two World Cups and
remains one of the greatest natural footballers the game has ever seen. His ability
to fly past defenders ensured the comparison
to a little bird stuck, and the name remained
with him for his whole life.

In one game in the 1958 World Cup against the USSR, having left a defender lunging desperately to the floor, he put his foot on the ball and offered his hand to help him up. Having hauled the Russian to his feet, he dribbled around him again and scampered off. Even in the biggest games of his career he would *nutmeg* a player, run around him, wait for his victim to catch up and then nutmeg him again for good measure. He was brilliant, and the fact remains that Brazil never lost a single game when both he and Pelé were on the pitch.

During my time at the BBC I once flew out to Brazil to film a pre-World Cup piece about the history and brilliance of the country's national side. During filming, the great Garrincha agreed to take a series of free kicks against me. It wasn't a great idea on reflection, as one shot after another flew past the flailing BBC presenter!

Garryowen

[rugby union] – *a very high up-and-under kick*

The idea of this move is that, if high enough, it gives the kicker sufficient time to run forward and put all his colleagues back on side, which allows several of them to compete for the ball as it comes down. It takes its name from *Garryowen* Football Club in Limerick, Ireland; the rugby club that invented the tactic some time after it was founded in 1884.

The term has more recently been adopted by the game of football for teams that don't play the ball on the ground. It's usually applied to desperate teams that, through lack of strength in midfield, resort to hitting the long and high ball from the back to a lone striker.

Gaylord flip

[gymnastics] – *a move that comprises a one-and-a-half front salto over the high bar before grabbing the bar again*

This internationally recognised move takes its name from the American gymnast Mitch *Gaylord*, who first performed it in competition in 1978. Gaylord later led the US team to an Olympic gold medal in 1984 and was the first American in history to receive a perfect 10. Since retiring from the sport, he has appeared in  several Hollywood movies, including *Batman Forever* (1995), for which he had to draw on his gymnastics skills as Chris O'Donnell's stunt double in the role of Robin.

To this day, the *Gaylord flip* and the even more elaborate *Gaylord II* are still regarded as two of the most formidable and spectacular accomplishments in the sport.

getting spoons

[rowing] – *a crew being hit or overtaken in four consecutive races in the Oxford and Cambridge University Bumps*

The *wooden spoon* – given as a notional award for coming last in an event – originated at Cambridge University in the early 19th century. The Mathematics student that got the lowest mark in their exam but still earned a third-class degree used to receive an actual wooden spoon as a booby prize for their dubious achievement. This custom lasted until 1909 when the system was changed so that the exam results were given in alphabetical rather than score order, making it impossible to tell who had come last. Nevertheless, the concept of the wooden spoon was established.

In the Bumps races, a number of boats chase each other in single file, with each boat trying to hit the boat in front without being bumped from behind. If a boat manages to hit the boat in front it will be promoted to that starting position in the race the following day. By the end of the week, the ultimate aim of a crew is to progress to the front starting position, or *Head of the River*. This is traditionally celebrated by the crew and its boat club by the burning of one its old boats. It also entitles the winning crew to commission trophy oars in their college colours with the names and weights of the successful crew on them. These are known as the *winning blades*. However, if a crew is bumped on every single day and as a result find themselves at the back of the pack at the end of the week, then they are awarded a wooden spoon, or are said to be *getting spoons*.

God

[football] – *a nickname for the great Dennis Bergkamp*

According to legend, the *Flying Dutchman* is a ghost ship that can never go home, but is doomed to sail the seven seas for all eternity. Nevertheless, its name has lent itself to a number of Dutch footballers over the years, including my friend Dennis Bergkamp. However, after an incident at the World Cup in 1994 when a journalist sharing a flight with the Dutch side said he had a bomb in his bag and Dennis decided that he didn't want to fly anywhere anymore, the name became somewhat obsolete. Journalists instead toyed with the *Non-Flying Dutchman* for a while before moving on to the *Iceman* and the *Dutch Master*. However, it's no coincidence that his time at Arsenal has coincided with his major strike partners breaking the club's scoring record, not once, but twice, and so, based on his ability to see things no-one else can, many Arsenal fans have ended up simply calling him God.

Of all the great footballers that have played for Arsenal, I would place Dennis at the top. Until his arrival players were coached to pass a ball with only a certain degree of pace and weight. Nevertheless, he gave everyone at the club something to aspire to, having raised the bar of a player's ability to control a football to a whole new level.

Golden Bear

[golf] – *a nickname for the great Jack Nicklaus*

He acquired this moniker as a result of his golden yellow hair. However, earlier in his career – until he lost weight in his thirties and established the true extent of his brilliance as a golfer, and consequent respect and admiration from the public – he was often referred to as *Ohio Fats* or *Fat Jack*.

Outside my football heroes, the *Golden Bear* is my favourite sporting icon.

golden goal

[football] – *a goal scored in extra time that instantly decides the match winner*

This rule was introduced to encourage attacking football and ultimately reduce the number of penalty shoot-outs. Other sports use the term *sudden death* for this rule, but the Fédération Internationale de Football Association (FIFA) – upon introducing the new rule at the European Championship finals in 1996 – decided to call it the *golden goal*, as sudden death was deemed too negative. In 2002, the Union of European Football Associations (UEFA) introduced the *silver goal* as well, whereby the team leading after the first fifteen minutes of extra time would win. After the European Championship finals in Portugal in 2004, however, both were removed from the laws of the game. This is a shame in my view, as I still think that the golden goal is a better and fairer way of settling finals than a penalty shoot-out.

golden sombrero

[baseball] – *the dubious feat of striking out four times in a single game*

This derives from the term **hat-trick**, which in the game of baseball was once reserved for a player who hit a single, double, triple and home run in the same game. Over time, however, it took on a far less positive meaning as it became a way of describing the ignominious achievement of striking out three times in a game. Since four is a larger number than three, the rationale of Don Baylor, the MLB stalwart who coined the phrase in 1989, was that it should be represented by a bigger hat, in this case a sombrero, which from above also looks like an awfully big zero.

A *platinum sombrero* or the *Olympic Rings* applies to a player striking out five times in a game, while a *titanium sombrero* is reserved for those who go one better and strike out six times in a single game. A titanium sombrero is also known as a *horn*, after Sam Horn, who accomplished the record feat while playing for the Baltimore Orioles in 1991.

golf

[golf] – *a sport played outdoors with clubs and a ball over a course of usually eighteen, but sometimes nine, holes*

The word *golf* is thought to have derived linguistically from the Dutch word *kolf,* meaning *club.* Kolf was a game played by the Dutch with a stick and ball on Holland's frozen canals in the winter. It's thought that Kolf reached the east coast of Scotland with Dutch sailors in the 14th century as a result of the considerable shipping trade between the two countries at the time. The Scots then adopted it, relocating it to the public grassy **links** on the coast, and over time it developed into the game we know today.

The first written reference to golf was in the statutes of the Scottish Parliament in 1457, when James II banned the sport because it interfered with archery practice and military training (this ban lasted until 1502). A number of similar bans of popular sports were made by James II of Scotland and several other monarchs, during that era of particular unrest with France (see also **cricket**).

Golf was spelt in a number of ways at that time, including *goff*, *goif*, *gouff* and *gowf*; before the invention of dictionaries, people largely wrote words phonetically, and that was how the Scots pronounced it. Only later, by the 16th century, did 'golf' become the common spelling that is still used today.

There are still a number of people who maintain that golf is an acronym for *Gentlemen Only, Ladies Forbidden*, but while there are still golf clubs that don't allow women members, this theory is untrue.

googly

[cricket] – *an off-break bowled with an apparent leg-break action in an attempt to deceive the batsman*

This type of ball is occasionally referred to as a *bosie* or *bosey*, after its inventor Bernard Bosanquet. He first revealed it jokingly during breaks in matches to amuse his fellow players. In time, however, it became regarded as a serious part of a leg-bowler's arsenal, mystifying batsmen so much that it made their eyes 'goggle'. The press then coined the term *googly* while Bosanquet and England were on a tour of Australia and New Zealand in 1902.

Asked by many at the time whether his googly might be illegal, Bosanquet replied: 'No. Only immoral.' This is perhaps why in Australia, to this day, it's still referred to as a *wrong'un*.

goose-step

[rugby union] – *a hitch-kick motion performed while running that makes the practitioner appear as if he is slowing down when actually he is speeding up*

The goose-step, still seen on different military parade grounds across the world and most commonly associated today with the German armed forces of the Wehrmacht, was invented by a British Army officer as a way of testing if any of his soldiers were drunk. Nevertheless, it lends its name to a move that became synonymous with the highest international try-scorer of all time, Australian David Campese, in the late 1980s. The former Australian coach Bob Dwyer wrote in his book, *The Winning Way*, of Campese's move: 'An Argentine defender had Campese well covered, but when he moved to tackle him, Campese did his famous goose-step. The change of pace deceived the Argentinean so comprehensively that he dived into touch, clutching thin air. The referee, the Welshman Clive Norling, was so impressed by this that he went up to Campese as soon as he had scored and told him it was the best try he had ever seen.'

Grand Prix

[motor racing] – *a type of race*

The first race to use this title was organised by the Automobile Club de France and run over two days at Le Mans in June 1906. It was won by the Hungarian-born Ferencz Szisz, who covered the 700 miles in a Renault at an average speed of 63 mph. Although today the term is most commonly associated with Formula One, it was initially used to describe the principal race in a region, whatever class of car it may have been – the drivers were contesting the *Grand* or *Big Prize*. After the end of the First World War, interest in motor sport grew rapidly. A series of *Grand Prix* races across Europe were reserved exclusively for Formula One before an annual Grand Prix calendar was put in place.

Grand Slam

[golf and tennis] – *the winning of all four major championships in the same year*

This term is borrowed from baseball, in which it denotes a home run hit when the team has a runner at each base and as a result scores four runs. There's a kind of reverse logic in that one swing of the bat with the bases loaded can achieve four runs, whereas in tennis and golf, a player has to win four tournaments in order to achieve the *Grand Slam*.

The term was first used for tennis in 1933 by American journalist John Kieran when describing the attempt that year by Australian Jack Crawford to win what have since become the four Grand Slam tournaments (the

Australian Open, French Open, US Open and Wimbledon).

The expression was later adopted fully by the golfing world, although someone is yet to win it with the current set of Majors (*Masters*, Open Championship, US Open and US PGA). Tiger Woods has come closest by holding all four simultaneously, only not in the same calendar year. This achievement has since been referred to as a *Consecutive Grand Slam* or a *Tiger Slam*. In tennis, it's possible to win the *Golden Slam* by winning the four Grand Slam tournaments as well as the gold medal for tennis at the Summer Olympics. This feat has been achieved only once – by Steffi Graf, in 1988.

The term has been taken up by a number of other sports over the years, including rugby union's Six Nations Championship, in which a team must win all of its five matches to secure the Grand Slam. However, rugby adopted the expression in the days of the Five Nations Championship, when only four wins were needed, making it true to its baseball origins.

The Graves

[golf] – *the 344-yard, **par**-4 2nd hole at Musselburgh Links, East Lothian*

Many historians believe Musselburgh is the oldest playing golf course in the world. Documents conclusively show that it was in use in 1672, although some say that Mary Queen of Scots played there as far back as 1567. If the following origin of the name of the 2nd hole is correct, then the course is older still.

On 10 September 1547, the Battle of Pinkie Cleugh was fought along the banks of the River Esk, near Musselburgh. It was the last battle to be fought between the Scottish and the English Royal armies and ended in catastrophic defeat for the Scots, with over half their army being captured, injured or killed.

It is thought that the 2nd hole at Musselburgh was chosen as a burial ground for many of the bodies as a way of discouraging future use of the course. Golf was deemed a distraction from military training by many at that time, and Pinkie Cleugh certainly seemed to substantiate that view. Nevertheless, golfers have played *The Graves* ever since.

Greco-Roman

[wrestling] – *a form of the sport in which only the upper body may be used for attacks*

This style of wrestling practised in Olympic and international amateur competition takes its name from its imitation of classical Greek and Roman representations of the sport. Thought to have originated with the ancient Greeks, it was then adapted and practised by soldiers throughout the Roman Empire 2,000 years ago.

Its most famous practitioner, Abraham Lincoln, was reputedly embroiled in a *Greco-Roman* bout when he was informed that he had been elected President of the United States in 1861.

Green Hell

[motor racing] – *a nickname given to the infamous 24-kilometre section of the Nürburgring by three-time Formula One World Champion, Sir Jackie Stewart*

The 'old' Nürburgring is one of F1's ghosts – a 176-corner nightmare winding itself around the medieval castle of Nürburg and the surrounding Eifel Mountains. F1 drivers used to disappear for over seven minutes into the fifteen miles of trees and hedgerows that made up the *Green Hell*. 'I was always relieved when it was time to leave', Jackie Stewart explained. 'The only time you felt good thinking about the Ring was when you were a long way away, curled up at home in front of a warm fire on a long winter night. You know, I never did one more quick lap there than I absolutely had to.'

Niki Lauda's fiery crash in 1976, when he had

to be pulled from the ***cockpit*** of his burning car by four of his fellow competitors who stopped to help, confirmed what everyone had known for years – the track was simply too long to marshall properly. Although it spelled the end for F1 through the Green Hell, it's still regarded by many as the greatest racetrack ever built and remains open today for any members of the paying public crazy enough to take it on.

Green Jacket

[golf] – *jacket worn by members of Augusta National Golf Club and awarded to winners of the **Masters**, which is played there*

This single-breasted jacket is coloured what is known as *Masters green*, and adorned with gold buttons and the club logo. It was introduced in 1937 and worn by club members during the Masters so that spectators could identify a reliable source of information. Although this practice continued, it was 1949 before what is now one of the most prized possessions in golf was awarded for the first time – the recipient was Sam Snead, the tournament champion for that year.

Group of Death

[football] – *typically the most unpredictable group of a tournament because of every team in it being roughly the same standard*

The term was coined in Spanish as *el grupo de la muerte* by Uruguay coach Omar Borrás at the 1986 World Cup in Mexico. He was anxiously describing Group E, which included Denmark, Scotland, Uruguay and West Germany. There was no real cause for concern, however, as the format of the group stage at that time meant that only one team was eliminated. Somewhat inevitably, some might say, Scotland caught the first plane home.

gully

[cricket] – *a fielding position on the off-side, almost square to the batsman at the end of a slip cordon*

It's thought that Arthur Owen Jones invented this position in the 1880s while still at school, before he went on to play for and then captain England. Its name comes from the word *gully* in its everyday sense, suggestive of the channel left between the slips and the point before a player was positioned there.

As it's principally a catching position, another suggestion is that the term comes from the 16th-century word *gull* meaning *gullet* or *throat*, whereby a player fielding there should *swallow* the ball when it comes to them.

Gunners

[football] – *the nickname for Arsenal FC*

In late 1886, a group of workers at the Royal Arsenal Armament Factory in Woolwich decided to form a football team. They called it *Dial Square* after a section of the workshops in the middle of the factory, and played their first match on 11 December of the same year, beating Eastern Wanderers 6-0. A few weeks later, they renamed themselves *Royal Arsenal,* and in 1888 adopted their first crest. The design was based predominantly on the coat of arms for the Borough of Woolwich and comprised three columns, which, although looking like chimneys, were in fact cannons.

After a few years of playing friendlies and entering local cup competitions, 1891 saw them become the first London club to turn professional – at the same time, changing their name to *Woolwich Arsenal.* In 1893, they also became the first London club to be admitted to the Football League. Starting off in the Second Division, they won promotion to the First in 1904. Despite this, their location meant lower attendances than other clubs, and so before long the club was in financial difficulty. In 1910, Fulham chairman Henry Norris took over Woolwich Arsenal with the intention of merging the two clubs. The Football League vetoed the idea, however, so Norris looked to relocate Woolwich Arsenal elsewhere. Initially sites in Battersea and Harringay were considered, before he finally chose the playing fields of St John's College of Divinity in Highbury. With the move, the Woolwich prefix was dropped and so the club became simply *Arsenal FC.*

In 1922, in the first match-day programme of the season, the club revealed a new crest; an east-pointing single cannon accompanied by the inscription, *The Gunners.* The design was amended again in 1925 to a slimmer and westward-facing cannon, but the inscription remained. Although the cannon then went largely unchanged until 2002, when it was pointed back east, the inscription had disappeared by 1949 – it was no longer required. Gunners had become the nickname for what is, without question, the greatest football club in the world!

guttie

[golf] – *an old-fashioned type of golf ball*

Preceded by the *featherie*, a hand-sewn leather golf ball filled with tightly packed animal feathers, and the wooden golf ball before that, the *guttie* takes its name from gutta-percha, the strong, waterproof, rubber-like dried sap of the Malayan gutta tree (*pictured*). The guttie was then succeeded at the beginning of the 20th century by the *Haskell*, the one-piece rubber-cored ball invented by American dentist Coburn Haskell. In 1905, Englishman William Taylor applied the first dimple pattern to the outer casing of a Haskell and the golf ball took on the form we know and still use today.

gymnastics

[gymnastics] – *an artistic sport performed on various pieces of apparatus*

In ancient Greece, male athletes trained and competed in the nude. The name *gymnastics* comes from the ancient Greek *gymnos* meaning naked, or *gymnazein*, which means to exercise in the nude. As a result, women were excluded from the ancient Games, both as competitors and spectators. Shame!

Hail Mary

[American football] – *a high and long pass thrown into or near the end zone without targeting any receiver in particular*

This is often used in desperation as a last resort at the very end of a game when there is only time for one more play and only a touchdown will do for the trailing side in possession. The quarterback will throw the ball towards a group of receivers in the hope that one of them will catch it and score.

The term was coined by Dallas Cowboys quarterback Roger Staubach during an interview after an NFC divisional playoff game with the Minnesota Vikings on 28 December 1975. With seconds of the game remaining, Staubach hurled a desperate 50-yard pass which found wide receiver Drew Pearson who just about managed to catch it and pin it against his right hip. Cornerback Nate Wright – who was covering Pearson – tripped over the receiver's leg, allowing Pearson to stroll into the end zone for the winning touchdown.

When asked about the play after the game, Staubach said that he had closed his eyes, thrown the ball as hard as he could and said a *Hail Mary* prayer.

hairpin

[motor racing] – *a 180° corner*

The hairpin corner is so called because from overhead it resembles the traditional thin double-pronged bobby pin used to fasten the hair. Probably the most famous hairpin in the world is *Rascasse*, the penultimate corner at the legendary Circuit de Monaco. Seven-time Formula 1 World Champion and five-time Monaco **Grand Prix** winner, Michael Schumacher, did nothing to diminish the corner's fame in his last ever appearance at the circuit in 2006, when he used it to perform one of the most suspicious manoeuvres in the history of F1. Provisionally on *pole* and with the qualifying session drawing to a close, Schumacher 'parked' his Ferrari at Rascasse, blocking the track and ensuring no one behind him could improve upon their time. In spite of his claims that it was a genuine mistake, the FIA didn't see it that way and sent him to the back of the grid where he joined his team-mate, Felipe Massa, making it the first time in the history of the sport that the two Ferraris would start the race on the back row.

haka

[rugby union] – *a traditional Maori war dance performed by the All Blacks before the start of a match*

According to Maori mythology, Tane-rore, the child of the Sun God and the Summer maid, created the *haka* that was then performed in different forms by warriors before going into battle. 'Haka' is the general term for Maori dance, and a version of this, the *Ka mate*, was first performed by the **All Blacks** in 1905. A hundred years later, at a Tri Nations match against South Africa in 2005, they unexpectedly introduced a new and much more aggressive haka called *Kapa o Pango*, which concludes with an ominous throat-slitting action directed at the opposing team. It will not act as a replacement for *Ka mate*, but instead will be reserved for 'special occasions'. I think it remains the most spectacular and intimidating piece of psychological warfare within the sporting arena.

Hammers

[football] – *a nickname for West Ham United FC*

In 1895, the foreman of the shipbuilding department of Thames Ironworks suggested to the Managing Director, Arnold Hills, the possibility of the company forming its own football club. Hills – keen to improve morale in his workforce in the wake of a bitter industrial dispute with his employees – thought it was a good idea and established Thames Ironworks FC. By 1898, they had turned professional and been elected to the Southern League.

In 1900, having acquired another engineering firm, Hills and the board decided to make Thames

Ironworks a public company. Consequently, with shareholders to consider, they could no longer carry on pumping the company's money into the football club. Thames Ironworks FC was subsequently disbanded but, in its place, West Ham United Football Club Company Limited was formed.

By that stage Thames Ironworks FC had become known simply as the *Irons*, a name that carried over to the formation of West Ham and the name by which fans still refer to their club today. Over time, journalists created the name *Hammers* as another reference to their Ironworks origins, not as an extension of the word *Ham*, as is sometimes thought.

hand of God

[football] – *the name given by Diego Maradona to his infamous hand-ball in 1990*

Four years after the Falklands War, Argentina and England met in the 1986 World Cup quarter-finals. Animosity was rife, with some fighting among the 114,580 fans in Mexico City's Aztec Stadium. Six minutes into the second half with the score still 0-0, Maradona played a one-two with team-mate Jorge Valdano on the edge of the box. England's Steve Hodge intercepted the ball but failed to clear it, accidentally looping it up towards goalkeeper Peter Shilton and into the path of the advancing Maradona. Now it doesn't take a genius to work out that at 6′1″, Shilton should be able to punch the ball comfortably clear over a 5′6″ Maradona trying to head it. Instead Maradona, by using his hand, beat Shilton in the challenge, scoring a goal and giving Argentina a 1-0 lead.

Covering the World Cup for BBC TV, I had an initial struggle to convince my colleagues that Maradona had used his hand. I was accused of supporting Peter Shilton, by being a member of the goalkeepers' union. We were watching it in a studio on the top floor but quickly ran downstairs to the videotape room in the basement, where the replay soon came to my rescue.

At the post-match press conference, Maradona claimed that the goal was scored 'a little bit by the *hand of God*, another bit by the head of Maradona'. For quite some time, the English press referred to it as the 'hand of the Devil'. More recently, in his 2002 autobiography, Maradona wrote, 'At the time I called it "the hand of God"', going on to admit proudly that this was nonsense, as 'it was the hand of Diego! And it felt a little bit like pickpocketing the English.'

Hands of Stone

[boxing] – *a nickname for Panamanian Roberto Durán*

Roberto Durán is one of the greatest lightweight boxers of all time. Although only 5'7", he had a frighteningly strong punch that saw him win his first world title aged just 21. Legend has it that even as a fourteen-year-old boy his punch was so hard that when a friend dared him to hit a horse, he knocked it unconscious. By the time he finally retired in January 2002, aged 50, his punch had gained him the nickname *Manos de Piedra*, or *Hands of Stone*.

hare

[athletics] – a pacemaker

Like the hare at a greyhound track, the principal role of a pacemaker is to act as something to chase. A good pacemaker will be employed to establish a fast speed and rhythm for the prevailing pack early in the race before naturally dropping back because they set a pace they can't sustain. In theory this allows the stars of the show to go on and win. Nevertheless, it hasn't always worked out like that.

At the beginning of the 1980s the British ruled middle-distance running. Sebastian Coe and Steve Ovett lorded over the 1,500 metres and spent much of the summer of 1981 avoiding each other on the track. Later in the year, with Coe absent in a race in Oslo, Ovett (who'd set a world record in the same event on the same track the year before) figured he'd win easily, despite squaring off against a field that included Steve Cram and John Walker.

On the first lap, pacemaker American Tom Byers surged out in front and by the start of the second was ten metres ahead of the prevailing pack. Ovett and company decided he was going too fast and – knowing he couldn't keep it up for long – let him go. By the end of the second lap he was 40 metres ahead. The others assumed he had lost his mind and by the start of the final lap had allowed him to open up a 70-metre gap. The chase began. By the home straight Ovett had cut the American's lead in half and despite the Englishman ripping through his last lap in 52.3 seconds, it still saw him cross the line half a second behind the exhausted hare.

'I don't think they'd let it happen again', said Byers.

hare and hounds

[cross-country running] – *a type of race*

Although man has run since the beginning of time, cross-country running did not evolve as a sport until the 17th century. It came about in England as a result of the wealthy aristocracy wagering bets on the outcome of their servants racing on foot across their vast areas of land.

By the 19th century, it had become much more widespread as a sport, especially in English public schools where they had developed *hare and hounds*, or *paper chases*. In these races, an individual, or *hare*, would set off, throwing little pieces of paper as he went, providing a trail or *scent* for his fellow pupils, or *hounds*, to follow. This concept is still practised by running clubs across the world today, although many now use flour instead of paper. However, this caused alarm during the anthrax scares in 2001, and so the hares in many city-based running clubs now mark the pavement or road with a piece of coloured chalk instead.

hat-trick

[cricket] – *the feat of taking three wickets with consecutive balls*

Although this term has now spread to other sports (notably football, for which it denotes that a player has scored three goals in a single match), its origin is in the game of cricket. In 1858 during a match at the Hyde Park ground in Sheffield, the bowler H.H. Stephenson – playing for an All-England XI – took three wickets with consecutive balls. It was customary at the time to reward outstanding sporting feats, so a collection was taken and used to buy a hat for Stephenson.

In time, this practice and expression made its way across the Atlantic to 1940s Toronto, where a haberdasher would award a free hat to any Maple Leaf ice hockey player who scored three goals in a game. This in turn led to the tradition still seen today at North American ice-hockey games, whereby fans shower the ice with their hats when a player scores a *hat-trick*.

haymaker

[boxing] – *an unrestrained punch usually leading to a knockout, whereby the fist is swung wide in an arc*

In the days of producing hay by hand, the worker or *haymaker* would slice at the grass with large swings of a scythe, causing it to fall to the ground in a heap. The term is thought to have entered the boxing lexicon at the beginning of the 20th century.

hector

[cricket] – *a box*

This comes from the following children's nursery rhyme about Richard Plantagenet, 3rd Duke of York, appointed Protector of the Realm when Henry VI (*pictured*) went mad in 1453:

Hector Protector was dressed all in green;
Hector Protector was sent to the Queen.
The Queen did not like him,
Nor more did the King;
So Hector Protector was sent back again.

Hell Bunker

[golf] – *718 square yards of sand on the
14th hole on the Old Course, St Andrews*

As the largest bunker on the course and at over 10
feet deep, its name speaks for itself. And similarly
to Hell, once you are in it, it's extremely difficult to
get out of – as the mighty Jack Nicklaus (or the
Golden Bear) found to his cost at the 1995 Open,
when he took four strokes to do so, scoring a 10 for
the hole.

Hell of the North

[cycling] – *a nickname for the famous 260-kilometre Paris–Roubaix one-day road race*

Started in 1896, the race is held annually in the mid-April rainy season, over the cobble-stoned roads and hard rutted tracks of northern France's coal-mining region. It has seen a number of horrific injuries over the years, but although fiercely difficult, this isn't how it acquired its nickname.

Immediately following the Great War, the course closely followed the largely abandoned front lines of battle and a consequent trail of devastation. Competitors cycled through mile after mile of ghostly ruins, trenches and rain-filled bomb craters and so to them, it was the *Hell of the North*.

Although the surroundings have been regenerated since then, the level of difficulty the course still poses means it has retained its name. Nevertheless, one man in particular has tamed it in its long and colourful history. Coming from a family of travelling clothiers, Belgian Roger De Vlaeminck, otherwise known as the *Gypsy*, entered the race fourteen times between 1969 and 1984 and never finished worse than seventh. He won the gruelling event a record four times, finished second four times and finished third once. All-in-all, a sufficient record to see him acquire the new moniker, *Monsieur Paris-Roubaix*.

hockey

[hockey] – *a sport played with sticks, a ball and two goals by two teams of eleven players*

Although historical records indicate that *hockey* has been played in some form or other for over 4,000 years, it was not until the mid-1800s that it acquired its current name. At this time, a Colonel named John Hockey, while stationed at the garrison on Fort Edward, Nova Scotia, used a game very similar to the one we know today as a way of keeping his soldiers conditioned. These workouts soon came to be known as playing *Hockey's game*.

Hogan Bridge

[golf] – *a stone footbridge that crosses over **Rae's Creek**, which runs in front of the green on the par-3 12th hole at the Augusta National Course*

The following words are written on a plaque at the bridge:

THIS BRIDGE DEDICATED APRIL 2, 1958, TO COMMEMORATE BEN HOGAN'S RECORD SCORE FOR FOUR ROUNDS OF 274 IN 1953. MADE UP OF ROUNDS OF 70, 69, 66 AND 69, THIS SCORE WILL ALWAYS STAND AS ONE OF THE VERY FINEST ACCOMPLISHMENTS IN COMPETITIVE GOLF AND MAY EVEN STAND FOR ALL TIME AS THE RECORD FOR THE MASTERS TOURNAMENT.

DEDICATED APRIL 2, 1958

Ike's Pond

[golf] – *a three-acre pond on the nine-hole course at the Augusta National Golf Club*

During his second visit to the Augusta National, General Dwight D. '*Ike*' Eisenhower went for a walk through the woods on the eastern part of the club grounds. On his return he informed the club's co-founder, Clifford Roberts, that he had found a perfect place to build a dam should the club ever want a fishpond. Soon after, the club did decide to build a pond and the architect heading up the project agreed exactly with Eisenhower's suggested location. Once built, it became known as *Ike's Pond*.

Imps

[football] – *a nickname for Lincoln City FC*

Formed in 1884, Lincoln City became a professional football club in 1891. The team takes its name from a twelve-inch tall gargoyle, high up in the east choir of Lincoln Cathedral. According to local legend, in the 14th century Satan sent two *imps* to Earth to conduct evil work. They first went to Chesterfield and twisted the church spire (see **Spireites**), before heading to Lincoln Cathedral. They started dancing on the altar, smashing up pews and tripping up the bishop, when suddenly an angel appeared. One of the imps cowered under a broken pew before making his escape. The other imp scampered to the top of a pillar and began to throw rocks at the angel. The irate angel turned the grinning imp to stone and it remains there to this day.

Indian dribble

[hockey] – *a dribbling technique whereby the player in possession of the ball pushes the ball rapidly from right to left and vice versa repeatedly while moving across the pitch*

In 1928, India entered a hockey team into the Olympic Games for the first time. They won the gold medal. In fact, they won the gold medal at the next five Olympics as well. During that era, India played 30 Olympic matches, winning all 30, scoring 178 goals and conceding only 7. They were, beyond any argument, the best team in the world. In 1956, they arrived at the Olympics with a new dribbling technique unlike anything the international hockey world had ever seen before. It helped ensure they won the gold medal without conceding a single goal. It was simply dubbed the *Indian dribble*, and is still the scourge of defenders to this day.

Invincibles

[football] – *the Arsenal side of 2003–04*

Between 7 May 2003 and 24 October 2004, Arsenal FC went 49 games unbeaten in the Premiership, amassing 121 points out of a possible 147. Although I know a few **Spurs** fans that will disagree, this record is unlikely to ever be surpassed. In the middle of that 596-day unbeaten run fell the whole 38-match season of 2003–04. They were *invincible* for an entire League campaign. But as I'm sure the same Spurs fans will be quick to point out, the term isn't exclusive to the mighty Arsenal. Several other teams have acquired the moniker over the years.

In 1982, the Australian national rugby league team toured Britain and France and won all 22 matches of their tour, running rampant and scoring 714 points while only conceding 100.

In 1948, a 40-year-old Don Bradman led the Australian cricket side on an unbeaten 32-match tour of England, which included a five-Test Ashes series which they won 4-0.

In 1924–25, the *All Blacks* toured England, Ireland, Scotland, Wales, France and Canada and returned home having won all 32 games and scored 838 points, while conceding only 116.

However, as far as Arsenal are concerned, I think it would be fair to say that they inherited the term from Preston North End, the only other team to have gone an entire season unbeaten in the top flight in the history of English football. Although their 1888–89 unbeaten season was sixteen games shorter than Arsenal's, that year Preston also became the first team to secure the Double, lifting the FA Cup without conceding a single goal! For that reason alone, they deserve their place in sporting history as the first ever team to be dubbed the *Invincibles*.

Iron Horse

[baseball] – *the nickname for Yankees legend, Lou Gehrig*

Until an aggressive form of motor neurone disease suddenly brought his career to an abrupt end in 1938, Lou Gehrig hadn't missed a single game in over fourteen years. He had played in 2,130 consecutive games, irrespective of any injuries he was nursing. Towards the end of the record-setting run, his hands were x-rayed, only to reveal seventeen different fractures that he had continued to play with throughout his career. His enduring reliability and consistency with the bat saw him nicknamed the *Iron Horse*.

In 1939, the Yankees **retired** Gehrig's number 4, making him the first sportsman in history to be afforded that honour.

jaffa

[cricket] – *an unplayable delivery*

A *jaffa* is a variety of orange originating in Israel. I'm not quite sure of the etymology here but would guess that (using the term *sweet* in its modern day sense as a way of describing something good) it's because the jaffa is sweeter than the average orange, just as the unplayable ball is 'sweeter' than the others in a bowler's spell. It is also thought that it derives from post-war Britain, when many people referred to oranges as *jaffas*, irrespective of the variety, and because of the food rationing of the time, a jaffa would have been rare, but exceptionally good when you finally got one.

jockey

[horse racing] – *a person who rides horses in races as a profession*

The word *jockey* is thought to have surfaced around the end of the 15th century, as an extension of the Scottish name *Jock* which was, and still is, a generic Scottish term for a man or boy. In the following century, 'jockey' began to be used to describe men of an untrustworthy nature, and in time, the verb *to jockey* came to mean *to outsmart* or *to get the better of.* Although this propensity to trick or cheat didn't necessarily apply to racers of horses at the time, their job was principally to manoeuvre their horse into an advantageous position within a racing pack by any means necessary, and perhaps some early jockeys employed underhand tactics to do so.

Apprentice jockeys always have an asterisk after their name in an official race programme to denote them as such. Because of the symbol's supposed resemblance to a bug, apprentice jockeys are known as *bug boys.*

join the dots

[cricket] – *to bowl cheaply*

A delivery which results in no score has always been marked down in the scorebook with a dot, and so is known as a ***dot ball***. If a ***maiden*** is bowled, the scorers will traditionally then use the two columns of three dots as a template for the two outer staves of the *M* that he or she will mark in the book at the end of the over. As a result, fielders sometimes try and motivate their bowlers by encouraging them to *join the dots*.

King

[golf] – *a nickname for the great Arnold Palmer*

This is born out of his popularity as a player and his achievements in promoting the game across the world. He began playing when he was four with a set of clubs cut down by his father and by 1967 had became the first man to reach $1 million in career earnings on the PGA Tour. His powerful, attacking play won him seven majors during his career and his charismatic approach to the game was a key factor in establishing golf in the 1950s and 1960s as a compelling television event. He is also credited with helping the Open Championship secure the status it holds today, after back-to-back victories at Birkdale and Troon in 1961 and 1962 inspired a wave of US players to make the trip across the Atlantic to compete for the ***Claret Jug*** in the following years. Unfortunately the consequence of that is that they seem to win it a little bit too often these days!

King of the Mountains

[cycling] – *the leader on points accumulated in the mountain stages of the Tour de France*

In the Tour de France, points are awarded for the first rider over the top of each mountain. Every climb through the Alps and Pyrenees is rated for difficulty, from the easiest, *Category Four*, through to *Hors Categorie*, which means *outside category* – so unpleasant it's beyond classification! The rider with the most points gained through this section of the race is recognised as *King of the Mountains*. This esteemed classification was first recognised in 1933 and won by Spaniard Vicente Trueba. The winner is sometimes also affectionately referred to as the *Mountain Goat* for his ability to climb.

In 1975, Tour organisers introduced and awarded the *polka-dot jersey* to the King of the Mountains in order to distinguish him from other riders. The design was based on the polka-dot wrapping of Poulain chocolate bars, the sponsors of the race at that time. During their tenure through the 1970s and 80s, the confec-tioner awarded each winner their own weight in chocolate!

lacrosse

[lacrosse] – *a sport played with a ball, long-handled sticks with a webbed pouch on one end, and two goals, by two teams of ten players each*

Originally, around the end of the 15th century, the game was developed by North American indigenous peoples, as a way of training for war. They called it *baggataway* and played it on a huge pitch half a kilometre long. It was violent and, although there were few fixed rules, each tribe made a point of having their own slight variation. The Cherokee tribe played it with hundreds of people on each side and, true to its initially intended purpose, knew it as the *Little Brother of War*. It was later adopted as a sport and given its modern name by French settlers in the area. *La crosse* is French for a *bishop's crozier*, which is what the sticks used in the game resembled.

lanterne rouge

[cycling] – *the overall last-place rider in a stage race*

This is French for *red light*, alluding to the one found on the back of a train. In more prestigious races such as the Tour de France, the label of *lanterne rouge* carries more kudos and considerably more publicity and, as a consequence, more money-making potential than

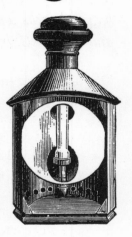

the rider who comes second from last. As a result, some riders in the past have been suspected of engineering themselves into last place in the closing stages of the race.

level pegs

[miscellaneous] – *either the same standard or score*

This is thought to have entered the sporting lexicon from the card game of cribbage via the game of darts. When the latter first began to be played in public houses over a century ago, the absence of the chalkboard or digital counter that you would usually find today meant players used the pegs in a cribbage board to score their match instead. When the scores were equal, the pegs were level, and so if anyone unable to see the small board wanted to know the score then the response would be that it was *level pegging* or *level pegs*.

links

[golf] – *a course on low-lying ground on the coast*

Coming from the Anglo-Saxon word, *hlinc*, meaning *ridge*, this has come to mean a rough grassy area that links the land and sea. True links courses are therefore those by the sea where the soil is sandy and where the grass has short blades but long roots. Scotland has many such areas, which are useless for agriculture but ideal for golf (especially in winter) because drainage is good. They were also away from towns and villages, meaning that, when golf was banned by James II from 1457 to 1502, people could still play without any prying eyes seeing them. The same applied when play on the Sabbath was banned from 1580 to 1724.

Lions

[football] – *the nickname for Millwall FC*

Millwall Rovers was founded in 1885 by workers at Morton's jam factory on the Isle of Dogs. Although thrashed 5-0 in their first game, the side went unbeaten in their next twelve games and soon established a band of support. The club's location on the Isle of Dogs inevitably meant that a large proportion of their supporters worked in the area's docklands. Over the coming years this saw the team become known as the *Dockers*.

However, in 1900, the team reached the semi-final of the FA Cup and a newspaper journalist – so impressed with their acts of giant-killing while getting there – referred to them as the *Lions*. The club liked it and adopted it as their name, as well as a lion emblem bearing the legend *We Fear No Foe*. In 1910, the club then moved to a new stadium that they named the *Den*.

Lions

[rugby union] – *a touring side comprising players from the British Isles*

Lions rugby began in 1888, when sporting entrepreneurs Arthur Shrewsbury and Alfred Shaw, having already taken an English cricket side on a tour of Australia, decided to move on to rugby. Although they successfully took a team of British and Irish players to Australia in 1888, the first official tour – whereby a committee from all four Home Unions picked the squad – was for a South Africa tour in 1910, by which time they were called the British Isles Rugby Union Team. This name remained until the tour of 1924, again to South Africa. They set out with their somewhat cumbersome title intact, but returned as the Lions – the new moniker chosen by the players because of the lion standing proudly above the crest on their official ties.

Little Master

[cricket] – *a nickname for Indian legend, Sunil Gavaskar*

Sunil Gavaskar is arguably the best opening batsman of all time. He gained the affectionate title of the *Little Master* due to his 5′4″ height and his phenomenal powers of concentration while demonstrating almost flawless technique. He scored 34 Test centuries in his career and was the first player to score more than 10,000 Test runs.

Little Tin Idol

[football] – *the original FA Cup trophy*

The current trophy is in fact the fourth in the history of the competition. The first, less than 18 inches tall and much smaller than the one in use today, was made by Martin, Hall & Co. at a cost of £20. It was first awarded in 1872 and remained in use until its theft in 1895. Holders Aston Villa had decided to exhibit the trophy in the window of a football outfitters shop in Birmingham, but the first night of its display, the shop was broken into and the Cup stolen. In spite of a £10 reward, it was never recovered and was assumed to have been melted down. Before its disappearance and despite it being made of solid silver, it had become popularly and affectionately known as the *Little Tin Idol*.

Although the trophy was never recovered, the story has an intriguing final twist. In 1958, 63 years later, an 83-year-old resident of a Birmingham hostel for the homeless named Harry Burge claimed that he had stolen it and used it to produce counterfeit half-crown coins. Although impossible to prove Burge's story, it remains the only plausible explanation for the Little Tin Idol's fate.

local derby

[football] – *a fixture between rivals from the same district*

Although this term is most commonly used for football, it can be applied to any sport. It's thought to have originated with a tradition started in the Elizabethan era in the town of Ashbourne in *Derbyshire*, a few miles from where I was born in Chesterfield. Each year, on Shrove Tuesday and Ash Wednesday, the people of the town board up shop windows and take to the streets to play the largest football match in the world. Although it is called the Ashbourne Royal Shrovetide Football Match, a fairly brutal game of rugby with fewer rules and a round ball might be a more accurate description. One team is made up of those born on the north side of the Henmore River, otherwise known as the Up'ards, and the other of those born on the south side – the Down'ards. The game kicks

off at 2 pm and is then played
until 10 pm on a pitch three
miles long. As if that wasn't
enough, much of it is played
out in the cold waters of the
Henmore, including the two
goals, which were originally
the wheels at the two local
mills.

In my twelve years at
Arsenal, there were rarely
more important, competitive
or violent encounters than our
local derbies with **Spurs**, our North
London rivals. Victory for one or the other was
hugely important for both players and, of course,
the fans, in what is always referred to as the *North
London derby*.

Long John

[golf] – *a nickname for John Daly*

Daly joined the PGA Tour in 1991 and as a rookie was the ninth and final reserve for a starting place in the USPGA later in the year. However, a series of late withdrawals saw the big man have to make a last-minute dash from his home in Arkansas to the Crooked Stick course, Indiana, where he shot a first-round 69 without even having time for a practice round. Daly's ability to hit the ball phenomenal distances off the tee with his driver played a huge part in his taming of the 7,200-yard course. He went on to shoot a 67, 69 and 71, winning him the tournament by three strokes. *Long John* had pulled off perhaps the most amazing win in the history of Major Championship golf.

Long Room

[cricket] – *the famous room at **Lord's** Cricket Ground, which every player must go through before entering the field of play*

When English architect Thomas Verity built the Lord's Pavilion in 1889–90, he had already designed the Criterion Theatre, the Comedy Theatre, and assisted in the design of the Royal Albert Hall. He knew how to design a building as a viewing area and the Lord's pavilion was no exception.

As a result, he designed the *Long Room*, in which three walls are now adorned with the portraits of people like Lord Harris, Douglas Jardine and W.G. Grace, and the length of one wall is made up almost entirely of windows with a view directly out onto the square. It's at this window that MCC members have sat on their high stools for well over a century, dishing out advice to batsmen as they pass through the room on their way out to face the music.

My only experience of the Long Room came in a charity debating event. Although an intimidating venue, there's no question that it's an inspiring one as well, and I wittered on passionately about my goalkeeping hero, Manchester City's German prisoner-of-war Bert Trautmann.

As its name suggests, it's a big room, the sort of place you shouldn't miss when making your way around the Lord's Pavilion. That didn't stop David Steele holding up proceedings in the 1975 Lord's *Ashes* Test however, when, descending from the dressing room to go out to bat on his England debut, he missed it entirely and found himself in the basement toilets.

Lord Byron

[golf] – *a nickname for the great Byron Nelson*

In 1945, Texan Byron Nelson won eighteen PGA tournaments. This included a streak of eleven consecutive wins – a record that remains to this day and one very unlikely to ever be beaten. He also finished second seven times, was never out of the top ten and at one point played nineteen consecutive rounds under 70. His scoring average of 68.33 for a single season remained a record for 55 years, he hit a record score of 62 for eighteen holes and a record of 259 for 72. 1945 is still regarded as the greatest single year by a player on the PGA Tour. The following year, he retired, aged only 34.

Nelson's swing was so consistent and perfect that 30 years later it was used as a model for a robotic machine to test clubs and balls for the USGA. Another 30 years on, it is still in use and named *Iron Byron* in his honour. Nelson also conducted his career with such gentlemanly conduct that the renowned Atlanta-based sports-writer O.B. Keeler nicknamed him *Lord Byron* after the famous English poet. Ken Venturi, a former pupil of Nelson's and one-time US Open winner also said: 'You can always argue who was the greatest player, but Byron Nelson is the finest gentleman the game has ever known.'

Lord's

[cricket] – *the Test cricket ground and home of the Marylebone Cricket Club in St John's Wood, London*

In the first half of the 18th century, the nobility played their cricket in Islington's White Conduit Fields, but as London's population grew, so did the players' impatience with the large crowds that appeared to watch. Looking to move elsewhere, they asked *Thomas Lord*, a bowler with White Conduit Cricket Club and an ambitious entrepreneur of the time, if he would be interested in setting up a new ground. Lord duly leased a ground on Dorset Fields in Marylebone, where he staged his first match on 31 May 1787 – and so the *Marylebone Cricket Club* (MCC) was born. A year later, the club produced a set of laws for the game, and to this day remains cricket's governing authority around the world.

MCC then moved to Marylebone Bank in Regent's Park for a short period between 1811 and 1814, before moving to a new rural ground in St John's Wood that previously had been the site of a simple country duck pond. This is still, however, the site on which *Lord's* cricket ground – the spiritual home of cricket – stands to this day.

Louisville Lip

[boxing] – *a nickname for the great Muhammad Ali from his fighting days*

Cassius Marcellus Clay Jr. was born on 17 January 1942 in Louisville, Kentucky, and went on to become, in many people's opinion, the greatest heavyweight boxer the world has ever seen. Part of his armoury – accompanying his phenomenal physical power and speed in the *ring* – was an ability to unsettle other boxers through talk. He was a master at getting into an adversary's head, often overtly and accurately predicting the round in which he would knock his opponent out. Here are a few examples that helped earn him the nicknames *The Mouth* and the *Louisville Lip*:

'Frazier is so ugly that he should donate his face to the US Bureau of Wild Life.'

'I'll beat him so bad he'll need a shoehorn to put his hat on.'

'It's hard to be humble when you're as great as I am.'

'I am the greatest, I said that even before I knew I was.'

As well as this slightly disparaging nickname, he was and still is more commonly known as *The Greatest*.

I am three months older than Ali and our sporting heights more or less ran parallel, albeit mine on a lesser stage than the great boxer. When he fought Sir Henry Cooper for the second time, the bout was staged at Highbury, home of Arsenal, and Clay used our dressing room to prepare.

love

[tennis] – *no score*

Reputedly this comes from the 18th-century expression *to play for love of the game*, in which *love* acts as a substitute for *nothing*. Some also believe that it derives from the French word *l'oeuf* meaning *egg*, as the shape of the egg resembles the zero that the player has to their name.

Lucien Petit-Breton

[cycling] – *a pseudonym for Argentine cyclist Lucien Georges Mazan*

Born in Northern France in 1882, Lucien Mazan moved to Argentina with his parents when he was six. As a young man he won a bicycle in a lottery and never looked back – he was determined to race for a living. However, his father disapproved and was equally determined that he would do a 'real job' instead. This was very much like my own dad who refused to let me become a professional foot-baller until I had acquired a 'proper job' first. The young Mazan was forced to compete under the pseudonym of Lucien Breton so as to keep his occupation secret from his family. As if that wasn't annoying enough, he found out that there was already another professional cyclist with this name and so was forced to race as *Lucien Petit-Breton* instead. He went on to break the World Hour record with a distance of 41.11 kilometres. He also won the first edition of the Milan–San Remo, the Paris–Brussels, and the Tour de France in both 1907 and 1908, becoming the first person to do so twice. It was quite difficult to revert back to his original name after all that and so his pseudonym stuck until his death in 1917, during the First World War.

madhouse

[darts] – *double one*

This name is born out of the frustration felt by many players in the past, as they struggle to finish the game with their least favourite and most difficult double. Also, by finding yourself on a score of two, the only way that remains to finish the game is by hitting a double one and so, until you've done it, you are confined to the *madhouse*.

Madison

[cycling] – *a 50-km track race, with two teams of two riders competing for points during intermittent sprints*

This race is slightly peculiar in that, although all four riders go round the track simultaneously, only one rider from each team can compete at any one time. While one is involved in a sprint, their team-mate conserves energy by circling the top of the banked track before being propelled back into action by grabbing the sprinter's hand. This is known as a *handsling*.

The race takes its name from *Madison Square Garden* in New York City, where it was first contested in the 1930s.

Magical Magyars

[football] – *a nickname for the legendary Hungarian National side of the 1950s*

For some years the Hungarian, or *Magyar* side was kept under wraps behind the Iron Curtain, but the beginning of the 1950s saw it unleashed upon an unsuspecting world. Between 14 May 1950 and 4 July 1954, the side went unbeaten for 32 international games – a record that stands to this day. The *Golden Team*, as they were otherwise known, was essentially built around six *magical* players. Gyula 'Black Panther' Grosics in goal, József 'Cucu' Bozsik at halfback, Zoltán Czibor on the left wing and forwards Sándor 'Golden Head' Kocsis, Nándor Hidegkuti and the legendary Ferenc 'Galloping Major' Puskás. During their unbeaten run, they became Olympic Champions in 1952 and winners of the Central European International Cup in 1953. The same year, they thrashed England 6-3 at Wembley (making them the first foreign side to beat England on home soil). This victory had worldwide significance as it effectively ended England's 90-year-old mythical reign since the creation of Association Football in 1863 over all foreign sides outside the British Isles. They then thrashed them again 7-1 when they met them in Budapest a year later (which remains England's largest ever defeat). They swept everyone aside in the 1954 World Cup in Switzerland, including West Germany who they beat 8-3, but who they would then also eventually inexplicably lose to in the final, 3-2. Their 32-match run had come to an end but only as a result of a match that the Germans felt compelled to dub the *Miracle of Berne.*

The Hungarian Revolution in 1956 and the subsequent occupation by the Soviet Union ultimately led to the disintegration of the great national side, but not before the *Magical Magyars* had made a massive impression on me as a youngster. So much so in fact, that they still remain one of my favourite international teams.

Magnolia Lane

[golf] – *the driveway from the front gates to the clubhouse of the Augusta National Golf Club*

In 1857, Belgian physician and amateur horticultur-alist Louis Berckmans established a nursery on a 365-acre site in Augusta, Georgia. One of the first things he did on the site was to plant a long row of magnolia trees from seed. In 1930, Bobby Jones bought the nursery from the Berckmans family for US$70,000 and although much of it made way for the golf course, the magnolia trees were kept and became the positioning for the club's drive. Sixty-one of the beautiful 150-year-old trees remain to this day, forging a tunnel along the 330-yard driveway that eventually spills out in front of the brilliant white Augusta National clubhouse. The American two-time Major winner Johnny Miller once described the awe-inspiring journey along *Magnolia Lane* as 'the quickest laxative in golf'.

Magpies

[football] – *a nickname for Newcastle United FC*

When Newcastle United began playing at St James's Park in 1892 they wore red shirts and over those, jerseys of red and white stripes. To avoid confusion with neighbouring Sunderland, they needed to change their strip. At a club board meeting on 2 August 1894: 'It was agreed that the Club's colours should be changed from red shirts and white knickers to black and white shirts (two-inch stripe) and dark knickers.' At no point in those official minutes does it state why they selected black and white. Here are a few theories that have emerged over the years.

During the English Civil War, the Earl of Newcastle raised an army of volunteers on Tyneside to fight for the king. He assembled what would become the cream of the royalist infantry in the North. They wore black pants and hats, with black leather boots, belts and pouches and were known as the *Newcastle Whitecoats*, because of their coats of undyed wool. Over the following two years the Whitecoats, or *Newcastle's Lambs* as they were sometimes otherwise known, fought valiantly, securing much of the North. However, with the Scottish invasion of England in January 1644, Newcastle was faced with a war on two fronts and the Battle of Marston Moor six months later would prove too much. A combination of the Scottish Army in the North and a further three Parliamentarian armies attacking from the South saw Newcastle well and truly beaten. The Whitecoats ultimately fought to their deaths and it's perhaps for this heroic last stand that Newcastle's very own regiment and their signature black-and-white uniforms were honoured by Newcastle FC, exactly 250 years later.

Another theory is based on the close proximity of the city's Blackfriars monastery to St James's Park, and one of its 19th-century inhabitants, Dutchman Father Dalmatius Houtman. He was an ardent supporter of the team, spending much of his time at the ground. Some think that the club, inspired by the traditional black and white of his habit, adopted the colour scheme as their own.

Club folklore also talks of a pair of *magpies* that made their nest in the old Victorian Stand at St James's Park towards the end of the 19th century.

The team became so attached to them, and the supposed luck that a pair of magpies brings, that they insisted upon adopting the colours of the birds as their own.

However the decision was ultimately reached, this basic colour design of the home kit has remained resolutely unchanged since 1894, although the sock colour has occasionally changed from black to white over the years – notably during the Ruud Gullit era, who believed white was lucky. Either way, the black and white of their strip has seen them dubbed the *Magpies*.

Maiden

[golf] – *the legendary giant sand dune on the 172-yard, par-3 6th hole at Royal St George's*

Towering to the left above the green, the giant hill takes its name from the fact that as you walk down the 5th fairway, the dunes between the 5th and 6th holes look like a *Maiden* lying down.

Over a century ago, the tee was positioned so that in order to hit the green, you had to 'fly the Maiden' and go straight over her, the ball often becoming hopelessly stuck in ruts or crashing into the sleepers on her face. However, in 1904, the tee was moved nearer the sea. Although further away from the green, Bernard Darwin, the great golf writer and St George's club member wrote: 'There stands the Maiden; steep, sandy and terrible, with her face scarred and seamed with black timbers, but alas! we no longer have to drive her crown: we hardly do more than skirt the fringe of her garment.' Although she doesn't pose the problems she once did, she still looms as a potent reminder of many rounds she ruined in the past.

James Bond creator, Ian Fleming, was a keen member at Royal St George's. Although shot at Stoke Park for the film, the golf scenes he set in the book *Goldfinger* were played at *Royal St Mark's*, clearly a reference to his beloved course. This was confirmed by a reference by Bond to a giant sand dune called the *Virgin*.

maiden

[cricket] – *an over in which no runs were scored*

Although now considered old-fashioned in an everyday context, the word *maiden* was used to describe a young unmarried girl, who was consequently almost certainly a virgin. In other words, a *maiden over* is one that the batsman has not managed to deflower.

manhattan

[cricket] – *a bar chart used by statisticians showing the number of runs scored in each over of a game*

So called because the bars supposedly resemble the skyscrapers that dominate the skyline of *Manhattan*, New York City.

The scoring areas of a batsman or team during an innings are also often represented on a circular pie chart. The graphic strokes supposedly resemble spokes and the chart is consequently known as a *wagon wheel*.

A line graph is also often used to plot a run rate against the number of overs bowled. The line usually wiggles back and forth across the page and so the graph is known as a *worm*.

mankad

[cricket] – *a form of dismissal whereby the bowler removes the **bails** instead of bowling if the batsman at the non-striker's end backs up too far*

This type of run-out takes its name from Mulvantrai 'Vinoo' *Mankad*, one of the greatest all-rounders India has ever produced. He caused controversy on India's 1947–48 cricket tour of Australia by removing opening batsman Bill Brown in this fashion at the Sydney Cricket Ground (SCG) in the second Test. It was not the first time he had dismissed Brown in this way on the tour either; it happened in an earlier match against an Australian XI at the same ground, but on that occasion he warned Brown before running him out.

The Australian press were unforgiving, labelling Mankad's actions as outrageous and unsportsmanlike. However, some Australians saw it differently – including the great Don Bradman, who later defended Mankad in his autobiography:

> For the life of me I can't understand why the press questioned his sportsmanship. The laws of cricket make it quite clear that the non-striker must keep within his ground until the ball has been delivered. If not, why is the provision there which enables the bowler to run him out? By backing up too far or too early the non-striker is very obviously gaining an unfair advantage.

Some people even considered the warning that Mankad had given Brown before getting him out as one of the most sporting acts the SCG had ever seen.

So, whichever side of the fence you sit on with regards to the morality of Mankad's actions, if you are run out in this fashion, then you are the victim of a *mankad* or have been *mankaded*.

marathon

[athletics] – *a 26-mile, 385-yard race*

In 490 BC, the Ionian Greeks attacked and destroyed the Persian colony of Sardis. Persia responded immediately by invading Greece, where the considerably more substantial and better-equipped Persian army were met by the Greeks on the plains of *Marathon*. Despite the disparity in numbers and weaponry, the Greeks were victorious. The legend has it that Pheidippides, the best runner in Greece, then ran the 26 miles from Marathon to Athens and, upon announcing the good news, died on the spot from exhaustion.

At the birth of the modern Olympic Games in Athens in 1896, a long-distance run was incorporated that covered the route chosen by Pheidippides from the Battle of Marathon over two millennia before.

At the 1908 London Olympics, at the behest of Queen Alexandra, consort to Edward VII, the starting line of the race, originally chosen as the approach to Windsor Castle, was moved to the lawn so that Princess Mary and her children could see the start from the nursery window, adding a further 385 yards to the 26-mile race. The new peculiar length became standard in 1924 and is still in use today, prompting the marathon runner's tradition of ironically shouting 'God Save the Queen' upon passing the 26-mile mark.

married man's side

[darts] – *the left-hand side of a dartboard*

In 1936, prolific English novelist Rupert Croft-Cooke took time off from his fiction writing to compile a book about the game of darts – a pastime he loved. In it he wrote of the trouble for players trying for high scores and consequently always going for 20, but very often hitting the neighbouring 1 or 5 instead. If a player was to aim at the *married man's side*; the section on the left of the board that incorporated the 12, 9, 14, 11, 8 and 16, they wouldn't be likely to get less than 30 with their three darts, and so would probably post a reasonable although not outstanding score – the rationale being that a married man should always play safe.

mashie niblick

[golf] – *a century-old hickory-shafted club with a loft between a mashie and a niblick, similar to a modern 9-iron, only with a longer shaft*

The name for a *mashie* is thought to have come from the Old Scottish word *mash*, which was used in the past as another name for a sledgehammer. The link with the sledgehammer is in the action involved. With a *massé* in **snooker**, the cue is brought down in a sharp stab from above so as to impart spin to the ball, and there is a similar theory in how to get the most out of a mashie.

A *niblick* is another old-fashioned, deep-bladed club for lofted shots particularly from the sand and deep rough. The name is thought to have come from *nib*, which refers to the *nose* (or *toe* as it is now more commonly known) being shorter than on any other wooden-shafted club of the time.

Although now fairly obsolete, the mashie, the niblick and the composite club, the deep-grooved or dimple-faced *mashie niblick*, were once a popular inclusion in a lot of golf bags: 'If your ball is lying in an almost unplayable position, try one of these mashie niblicks!' exclaimed the Army & Navy catalogue of 1907. It was certainly my Scottish dad's favourite golf club, as by his own admission it was constantly getting him out of trouble!

Master Blaster

[cricket] – *a nickname for the great Sir Isaac Vivian Richards KBE*

'You knew he was coming', explains *Wisden*'s Mike Selvey. 'The outgoing batsman would already have disappeared into the pavilion, and the expectation of what was to follow filled the air. Viv kept you waiting … time to ponder. Then he appeared, sauntering, swaggering, arms windmilling slowly. He would take guard, and then, head tilted back slightly and cudding his gum, he would walk a few paces down the pitch to tap it while looking the bowler in the eye. It was calculated menace and magnificent theatre from arguably the most devastating batsman of all time.'

'Occasionally, for no apparent reason, he would block an over in immaculate fashion, seemingly in defensive position before the ball had left the bowler's hand. Then, refreshed, off he would go again.'

Playing England at St John's in 1986, Richards confirmed his moniker when he took just 56 balls to hit the fastest Test century the game of cricket has ever seen.

Masters

[golf] – *tournament played every spring at the Augusta National Golf Club*

In 1934, Bobby Jones and Clifford Roberts, co-founders of the club, organised the inaugural Augusta National Invitation Tournament. Roberts had wanted to call it the *Masters* but Jones objected, thinking it too presumptuous. It kept its initial name for another five years, until Jones eventually relented and it officially became the Masters in 1939.

Masters Club

[golf] – *a dinner held annually at the Augusta National Golf Club on the Tuesday of **Masters** week for all previous winners of the tournament, hosted by the defending Champion*

In 1952, defending champion Ben Hogan gave a dinner for the ten other previous winners of the Masters. At the dinner he proposed the formation of the *Masters Club*, with its membership limited only to champions of the tournament plus the Golf Club's co-founders, Bobby Jones and Clifford Roberts. It was agreed that the Masters Club would get together each year for a similar dinner on the Tuesday before the tournament and as a certificate of membership, the defending champion would be presented with a gold locket in the shape of the Club emblem. The tradition has taken place every year since and although the Augusta National still

officially refer to it as the Masters Club, it has more commonly become known as the *Champions' Dinner*.

As well as hosting the dinner, the defending champion gets to choose the menu. Players have used this opportunity to show off the culinary delights of their home nation over the years, notably Canadian Mike Weir who chose wild boar, Arctic char and Wapiti elk, and Sandy Lyle, the wonderful haggis, neeps and tatties!

Mendoza line

[baseball] – *a batting average around .200*

This is considered the lowest limit of respectability for a professional hitter. The term is thought to take its name from the former successful shortstop Mario Mendoza. Although Mendoza finished with a career batting average of .215, the 1979 season saw him record an average of .198.

It's thought that the term then originated with Kansas City Royals star George Brett who, when asked about his own average soon after, responded: 'The first thing I look for in the Sunday papers is who is below the Mendoza line.' It should also be noted that Brett was full of praise for Mendoza's defensive qualities but as far as his assessment of his batting was concerned, the phrase stuck and is still very much in use today.

metronome

[cricket] – *a fiercely consistent bowler*

So called because like the different settings on a *metronome*, the bowler will reliably hit the spot requested by his captain, over and over again. The term is often used to refer to seam bowlers – who consistently find the **corridor of uncertainty** – such as Glenn McGrath, or **Pigeon**, who former Australian captain Ian Chappell refers to as the 'Miserly Metronome'.

Michelle

[cricket] – *a five-wicket haul by a bowler in a single innings*

This is rhyming slang for the word *fifer*, a cricketer's contraction of the term *five-for*. It takes its name from the American Hollywood actress *Michelle* Pfeiffer.

Mick the Miller

[greyhound racing] – *probably the most famous greyhound of all time*

He was born in Ireland in 1926, bred by a parish priest. The runt of a litter of twelve, he contracted a particularly virulent strain of canine distemper and almost died. As he slowly recovered, the priest named him after *Mick Miller*, an odd-job man who worked at the vicarage and tirelessly helped nurture the puppy back to health. In 1928, the priest took the jet-black greyhound to London's White City Stadium for his first ever race. He won, and never looked back. He went on to win a phenomenal 61 of his 81 starts, including the Derby in successive years, a feat not repeated for nearly half a century. He is perhaps the greatest racing greyhound that ever lived.

Milky Bar Kid

[darts] – *a nickname for former World Champion, Keith Deller*

In 1983, Keith Deller became the first and still youngest ever qualifier to be crowned World Champion. On his way to the final he beat third seed John Lowe and then second seed Jocky Wilson, before meeting top seed Eric Bristow in the final. 'He's not just an underdog', said the commentator Sid Waddell of 23-year-old Deller: 'He's the underpuppy.' Needless to say, he won the final. He acquired his nickname from the character used to advertise chocolate bars throughout the 1980s – as a result of his age and his clean-cut image, and because he drank milk during his games.

Monkeyhangers

[football] – *a nickname for Hartlepool United FC*

According to local legend, a large French ship was wrecked off the Hartlepool coast during the Napoleonic Wars. The only survivor was a monkey, who was washed ashore clinging to some wreckage and dressed in a French military uniform – presumably to amuse the ship's crew. The locals quickly held an impromptu trial on the beach. Being a monkey, it obviously didn't respond particularly well to their questioning and so, with its supposed refusal to give up any information, the locals came to the conclusion that it was a spy and should be sentenced to death. The unfortunate creature was promptly hanged, the mast of a fishing boat providing the makeshift gallows.

The Hartlepool United FC mascot is called *H'Angus the monkey*. In 2002, the man in the monkey costume stood for Hartlepool mayor 'for a laugh', dressed as H'Angus and offering free bananas for schoolchildren if he won. He did, and with his victory quickly found himself overseeing a £106 million budget and over 3,000 staff.

mulligan

[golf] – *a free extra shot sometimes taken as a second chance in a social match*

There are several different stories that circulate as a possible origin of this word, three of which cite a Canadian golfer, David *Mulligan*. Mulligan was a successful hotelier of the time and played much of his golf at St Lambert in Montreal during the 1920s. The first story suggests that on one occasion, having hit a very long drive off the tee but not in the right direction, he placed another ball on the tee and hit that as well, explaining it to his friends as a 'correction shot'. They were amused by his behaviour but felt it deserved a better name and so called it a mulligan.

The second story tells of Mulligan's friends allowing him a free shot as a result of him having to drive them along the bumpy and windy road to the club that morning.

The third version is that he overslept and having rushed frantically to make it to the first tee in time, hit an awful drive, and so his friends let him have another.

Some also believe – although it seems unlikely as it occurred later than the other stories – that it takes its name from a John A. 'Buddy' Mulligan, a locker-room attendant at Essex Fells, New Jersey, in the 1930s. John Mulligan was well known for his propensity to replay shots, particularly on the first tee. Whichever story you believe, the term had gained widespread use on golf courses by the 1940s.

Murderer's Row

[baseball] – *a nickname given to the New York Yankees batting line-up of 1927*

Murderer's Row was a line of high-security prison cells at New York City's infamous 19th century Tombs prison. It housed condemned murderers and particularly violent criminals and lent its name to the World Series-winning Yankees batting order on account of them 'murdering' pretty much every pitcher that they met throughout their record-setting season of 1927, some of which remain to this day.

At that time games started at 3.30 pm and were often over by 6 o'clock, the Yankees line-up – which included the legendary Babe Ruth and Lou Gehrig – usually wrapping up proceedings in the late innings with the fatal blows that became known as *five o'clock lightning*.

musette

[cycling] – *a small cotton shoulder bag containing food that's handed to riders during a race*

Otherwise known by cyclists as the *bonk bag*, a *musette* takes its name from the French for a horse's nosebag. It's an essential item for a rider during a race because a lack of food will see their body run out of glycogen, the stored chemical the muscles burn for energy. In extreme cases, this can bring on a sudden state of delirium, known as the *bonk* or the *knock*, the equivalent of a marathon runner's *hitting the wall*.

nassau

[golf] – *a type of informal game consisting of a given bet for the front nine, a given bet for the back nine and a final bet for the overall game*

This game takes its name from *Nassau* Country Club in Glen Cove, New York, where it was invented in 1900. At that time, inter-club matches were in vogue, and teams from Nassau CC, as well as those from other exclusive clubs in the New York area, had many high-profile members who were often in the news of the day. Although prominent members of the club, they weren't always great golfers and would sometimes lose their games by embarrassing margins. In order to avoid scores like 9 and 8, the club captain John B. Coles Tappan devised a system whereby, if you lost the entire match, the worst possible result could only be 3-0. With many of the high-profile members happier with the new concept, it caught on and as it spread to other clubs became known as the *nassau* way.

Nelson

[cricket] – *the score of 111 or multiples thereof, considered unlucky by many cricketers*

111 is considered unlucky due to its resemblance to the three **stumps** with the **bails** missing. The name was coined thanks to the common misconception that Admiral Horatio *Nelson* had lost one arm, one eye and one leg in battle, whereas he had the use of both of his legs until his death at the Battle of Trafalgar in 1805.

There is an old superstition that originates from Gloucestershire, whereby to avoid being out while on Nelson, the whole team except the batsmen must keep their feet off the ground. Before his retirement in 2005, the great umpire David Shepherd could always be seen giving a hop on one foot until the score changed.

222 is known as *double Nelson*, 333 as *triple Nelson* and so on. The Australian equivalent of Nelson is the **devil's number**. This is any score that includes 87, which is thought to be bad luck as it's 13 short of a century.

Nelson Bridge

[golf] – *a stone footbridge that crosses over **Rae's Creek**, taking players from the 12th green to the 13th tee at the Augusta National Course*

The following words are written on a plaque at the bridge:

> THIS BRIDGE DEDICATED APRIL 2, 1958,
> TO COMMEMORATE BYRON NELSON'S
> SPECTACULAR PLAY ON THESE TWO HOLES
> (12–13) WHEN HE SCORED 2–3 TO PICK UP SIX
> STROKES ON RALPH GULDAHL AND WIN
> THE 1937 MASTERS TOURNAMENT. IN
> RECOGNITION ALSO TO GULDAHL, WHO
> CAME BACK WITH AN EAGLE 3 ON 13 TO
> GAIN WINNING POSITION IN 1939.

See **Lord Byron.**

nightwatchman

[cricket] – *a lower-order batsman sent in as an alternative to the scheduled, more skilled batsman, towards the close of play*

Some believe this to be an illogical practice – for example, Steve Waugh never employed the tactic in his tenure as Australian captain. But the rationale is that sending in a top-order batsman late in the day places them in a no-win situation; they can't achieve a great deal in the short time available, and if their wicket falls, it will have an even more detrimental effect on the team. Therefore, the lower-order batsman is sent in with the sole purpose of surviving until the end of the day so that he remains in overnight, returning with everything safely in place in the morning – hence his title, the *nightwatchman*.

Although the nightwatchman is called upon to play a predominantly defensive role, and as a result very little is expected of them in terms of runs, there have been a few notable exceptions to this. In 1988, England wicketkeeper Jack Russell was sent in as a nightwatchman on his Test debut against Sri Lanka at *Lord's*, but went on to score 94 – his then highest first-class score. Harold Larwood, when sent in at number four instead of his customary number nine against Australia in the ***Bodyline*** Series of 1932–33, scored 98. More recently, Alex Tudor, while playing for England against New Zealand and without a first-class century to his name, was sent in as nightwatchman with England needing 210 to win. He guided England to victory, remaining unbeaten on 99. In April 2006, Jason Gillespie surpassed the previous record of 105 set by fellow-Australian Anthony Mann against India in 1977, by making 201 not out against Bangladesh.

Nine Dart

[darts] – *a nickname for British Darts Organisation stalwart Shaun Greatbatch*

Nine is the fewest number of darts that a player can possibly throw to win a game of 501. It's the ultimate *checkout* (finish to a game) and notoriously difficult to achieve. In 1984, John Lowe became the first player to have a televised nine-dart finish, but it was in fact recorded from a game earlier in the day. At the Dutch Open in 2002, Shaun Greatbatch became the first player ever to do it live on television, subsequently earning him the nickname *Nine Dart*.

nineteenth hole

[golf] – *the clubhouse bar*

So called because it's usually the next destination for players after the 18th green. Although references to this term are evident from the very beginning of the 20th century, it's thought to have later been assigned a permanent place in the golfing lexicon by the work of P.G. Wodehouse, many of whose short stories were told through a fictional character on the terrace of the *nineteenth hole*.

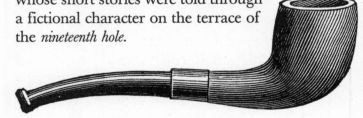

99 call

[rugby union] – *the infamous command of Willie John McBride MBE on the 1974 **Lions** tour of South Africa*

When Irishman Willie John McBride led the British Lions to South Africa in 1974, no one had ever beaten the **Springboks** on home soil. Not even the **All Blacks**, and they had been trying for the best part of a century.

In the early games of their tour, the Lions were victims of a series of premeditated assaults by South African players, with home referees apparently turning a blind eye. In spite of this, the Lions won the first two Tests but when South Africa picked No. 8 Gerrie Sonnekus to play at scrum half for the third Test, it didn't take a genius to work out what they had in mind.

The late Gordon Brown, the Scotland second-row forward, recalled the lead of his captain: 'We had a meeting about how to react [to the violence] and it fell to the big man to decide what to do. He took a long puff on his pipe, then he simply said, "From now on, boys, we get our retaliation in first". It was then that the "*99*" *call*, a cry to stamp out likely troublemakers, was born.'

It was decided that upon the hearing the words 'ninety-nine', each Lion would stop what they were doing and start fighting with the nearest South African to hand. 'There was method to the madness', McBride would later explain. 'You see, there were fights breaking out all over the place and some o' me lads were running 100 yards just to get a kick at a South African – retaliation like. Now that was no use to me. If someone like Gordon Brown, say, was fighting for 10 minutes that was 10 minutes he wasn't playing rugby. The "99 call" ensured everyone had a chance to settle their grievances and be ready to play 30 seconds later. Even a South African referee, so I reasoned, couldn't send off all 15 of us.'

McBride chose the 99 call as it was a shortening of 999 – the British telephone number for the emergency services.

no man's land

[tennis] – *the area of the court between the baseline and the service line*

It's usually inadvisable to find yourself in *no man's land* as you're too deep for a natural volley and not deep enough to receive a baseline return at a satisfactory height after it's bounced. The same principle applies for a goalkeeper in football when faced with a teasing cross. The speed of the lighter modern ball and its propensity to move about in the air have made decision making for the keeper even more of a problem than in my playing days. Even so, he should either commit to the ball and then make absolutely sure he gets there to claim it, or alternatively stay on his line and let his defenders deal with it. Anywhere in between is dangerous, and so takes its name from the far more dangerous unoccupied area of land found between enemy trenches during the First World War.

nutmeg

[football] – *a skilful move in which a player deliberately passes the ball through his opponent's legs and retrieves it on the other side*

A term that is thought to have been inspired by deceitful practice in the *nutmeg* trade during the Victorian era, whereby American exporters would cut their batches of nutmeg with similar looking bits of wood. The recipients deceived, or *nutmegged* as it came to be known, were left looking foolish, as is the victim of a nutmeg on a football field. In the current game, players affectionately use the term *nuts* when a team-mate or an opponent is on the receiving end of this skill.

oche

[darts] – *the line behind which a player has to stand when throwing darts*

This word was officially recognised by the British Darts Organisation only in the late 1970s. From the 1920s, the word *hockey* was used instead. Although the reason is unclear, it's thought that this came about because people used the crates from a West Country brewery called *Hockey and Sons* to

standardise the distance between the player and the board. The crates were two feet in length, so pubs used four of them to mark out the eight feet that was the standard distance for many years, and in some places, still is.

Over time, the *h* was dropped, so phonetically it became *ockey* and then acquired the new spelling, *oche*.

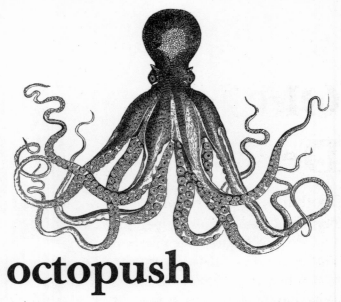

octopush

[octopush] – *a type of underwater* **hockey** *played in a 25-metre swimming pool with a lead puck, by two teams of ten – only six of whom are allowed in the water at any one time*

This game was invented by a group of subaqua divers in Southsea, England, at the end of the summer in 1954, in order to spice up the winter confined to diving in their local swimming pool. It soon spread to the United States, South Africa and Australasia.

According to its inventors, the rules of the sport were determined by the word *octopus*: originally it was to be played with teams of eight (*octo*) wielding sticks which they used to *push* the **puck** (or *squid*).

Old Farm Derby

[football] – *a fixture between Ipswich Town and Norwich City FCs*

The two sides met for the first time on 15 November 1902. **Local derbies** between the two clubs have become as important as one would expect from over a century's rivalry. Nevertheless, it's often referred to as the *Old Farm Derby*, a humorous reference to the **Old Firm** *Derby* between Celtic and Rangers, one of the oldest and most ferocious fixtures in world football. Similarly to Ipswich Town's recent acquisition of the nickname *Tractor Boys*, the reference to farming reflects the remote positioning of the two teams in the heart of agricultural Norfolk and Suffolk. They consequently play for the right to be called the *Pride of Anglia*.

Old Firm

[football] – *Celtic and Rangers Football Clubs*

The rivalry between these two clubs is one of the oldest and most ferocious in world football, going back to when they first met at Celtic Park in 1888, watched by around 2,000 fans. Today, this collective term for these two Glaswegian clubs is used principally as a short nickname – for instance, when they meet in a ***local derby***. However, when it was first used early in the 20th century, it was intended as a more scathing implication that the two clubs were in charge of Scottish football at that time, and ran it without consideration of other clubs. The term was chosen to signify the lucrative aspect of their frequent meetings, and the belief that the two clubs colluded to ensure their own profit and consequent domination, at the expense of the other Scottish clubs.

Whether this is true or not, no two teams across the world have dominated their national championship like Celtic and Rangers. As of 2008, between them they have won 92 of the 113 Scottish titles available since 1890.

Although I never knew him, a great uncle of mine – Sir John Ure Primrose – was Chairman of Rangers at the turn of the 20th century, and in 1902 he officially opened Hampden Park.

Old Mongoose

[boxing] – *a nickname for the legendary Archie Moore*

Archie Moore made his professional debut during the Great Depression of the 1930s, got his first title shot with the advent of TV, and didn't hang up his gloves until the outbreak of Beatlemania three decades later. He's the only man to have faced both Rocky Marciano and Muhammad Ali, fighting the latter one month and one year before his 50th birthday – an age that saw him nicknamed *Ancient Archie* and the *Old Mongoose*. His career tally of 145 knockouts is still a record and one that will perhaps never be beaten.

on the hoof

[rugby union] – *a player in action*

This phrase can only really be said properly by one man: its inventor and chief exponent – the great Bill McLaren. Before his illustrious career in commentating, which lasted more than 50 years, he was on the verge of playing for Scotland at flanker, when he contracted a form of tuberculosis that almost killed him. Needless to say, it brought his playing career to a premature end, but although the game lost out in one area, it gained immeasurably in another. While recovering from his illness, he began to commentate on table-tennis matches on the hospital radio, before going on to be the greatest commentator of rugby union the world has ever known. Although now retired, to the extreme detriment of the game, he will always be remembered for an endless number of catch-phrases, not least of all: 'Seventeen stones of Scottish prop *on the hoof*!' A wonderful man and a former BBC colleague – in short, a national treasure.

on the rivet

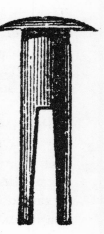

[cycling] – *to ride as fast as possible*

On old leather types of saddle, a copper rivet was used at the front to hold the leather in place. When riders are at their physical limit, they naturally sit nearer the front of the saddle and so are said to be *on the rivet*.

out of the screws

[golf] – *a big drive*

This expression goes back to the days when wooden drivers had four wood screws surrounding the middle of the clubface. If the ball came *out of the screws*, it meant that it came out of the *sweet spot* and so the shot invariably went a long way.

outjump the hill

[ski-jumping] – *to jump beyond the point where the landing area ends and the hill flattens out, otherwise known as the k point, or critical point*

In the past, ski-jumpers always kept their skis parallel in flight. In 1985, Sweden's Jan Boklöv suffered a mild epileptic attack while mid-jump, seizing his body and skis in the V position that has since been adopted by all professional practitioners of the sport across the world. This technique enabled jumpers to fly beyond the *k point* for the first time, and so Boklöv inadvertently made it possible to *outjump the hill*.

Oval

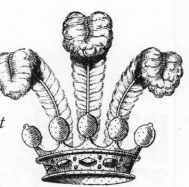

[cricket] – *a Test cricket ground in Kennington, London*

The *Oval* came about in the 1790s, when an oval road was built around what was then a cabbage patch. Subsequently, the land was turned into a market garden but was later closed through lack of interest. It became a sports ground in 1845 after 10,000 grass turfs were brought in from Tooting Common at a cost of £300. It staged the first FA Cup Final in 1872, the first England football international in 1873, the first England vs. Wales and England vs. Scotland rugby internationals in 1876, the first cricket Test on English soil in 1880, and the inaugural **Ashes** Test in 1882. Owned by the Prince of Wales, it certainly was and still is one of the most important sports grounds in the world.

pair of spectacles

[cricket] – *two **ducks** in the same match*

If a batsman has two zeros to his name in a game, they are said to resemble the lenses of a *pair of spectacles*. If a player loses his wicket on his first ball in each innings, then he has two *golden ducks* to his name – which constitute a *king pair*.

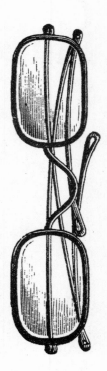

Palooka

[boxing] – *an inexperienced or incompetent boxer*

In 1930 American Ham Fisher started *Joe Palooka*, which ran until 1984, turning out to be one of the most successful comic strips of all time. Although the eponymous Palooka was a patriotic, likeable and morally sound heavyweight championship boxer of the highest quality, he wasn't particularly bright and so, over time, his name was somewhat unfairly adopted by the boxing community to represent an inexperienced or incompetent boxer.

par

[golf] – *the benchmark score for quality play on a specific hole or course*

Some believe that *par* is an acronym of *professional average result* – although given the word's history this seems unlikely. It was originally used on the stock exchange, where a stock may be above or below its normal or par price. It was used in a golfing context for the first time in 1870, when golf writer A.H. Doleman asked James Anderson and David Strath, two competitors for the Open Championship at Prestwick, what score would win it. They thought that 49 would be sufficient on Prestwick's twelve holes, which Doleman subsequently labelled as par. The tournament was then won by Young Tom Morris with a score of two over par.

In time, different governing bodies across the golfing world standardised par to represent the score which all golfers should try to equal, if not better.

Par 3 Fountain

[golf] – *the fountain found adjacent to the 1st tee on the Augusta National's par-3 course*

Every year since 1960, the Wednesday before the start of the *Masters* has seen the tournament participants, non-competing past champions and honorary invitees do battle in the Par 3 Contest over Augusta's 1,060-yard par-3 course. It is treated as a bit of fun and the last stress-free moment before the main event begins on the Thursday, with many participants letting their children *caddie* for them, signing autographs for the fans as they go round, and taking a *mulligan* when a shot goes in the water. Nevertheless, as no winner of the Par 3 Contest has ever gone on to claim the *Green Jacket* in the same year, some regard it as a jinx and in some cases play the last hole suspiciously badly. A list of all the winners can be found on the *Par 3 Fountain*, beginning with Sam Snead's inaugural victory in 1960.

perfume ball

[cricket] – *a bouncer on or just outside off-stump that passes within inches of the batsman's face*

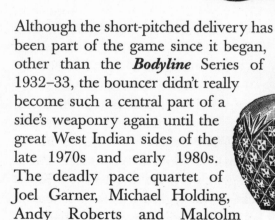

Although the short-pitched delivery has been part of the game since it began, other than the **Bodyline** Series of 1932–33, the bouncer didn't really become such a central part of a side's weaponry again until the great West Indian sides of the late 1970s and early 1980s. The deadly pace quartet of Joel Garner, Michael Holding, Andy Roberts and Malcolm Marshall would constantly fire in the *perfume ball* – so close to the batsman's face that he could smell it.

Pichichi

[football] – *the individual top scorer in La Liga at the end of the season*

Rafael Moreno Aranzadi, or *Pichichi*, as he was otherwise known, played for Athletic Bilbao during the 1910s and 1920s. He became a legend in Bilbao, scoring the first ever goal at the San Mamés Stadium (or *La Catedral* as the fans still call it today), before going on to win the Copa del Rey four times with the club. Tragically, in 1922, aged only 29 and in his prime, he died after contracting typhus.

In 1926 a bust was erected outside the stadium in his honour. Teams visiting the stadium for the first time still pay homage to Pichichi by leaving a bouquet of flowers at its base. In 1953, the Spanish sports newspaper *Marca* introduced the *Trofeo Pichichi* to be awarded to the top scorer at the end of each season. Over half a century later the trophy is still in use, and if you win it, you are simply known as Pichichi.

Pigeon

[cricket] – *a nickname for Glenn McGrath*

Glenn Donald McGrath is one of the most highly regarded bowlers in the history of the game and has played an essential role in Australia's domination of world cricket for over ten years. He's taken more Test wickets than any other fast bowler who has ever graced a cricket pitch. Needless to say, this doesn't grant him immunity from the nickname of *Pigeon*, which he acquired from teammate Brad McNamara while playing for New South Wales. 'You've stolen a pigeon's legs, McGrath!' exclaimed McNamara upon seeing his spindly pins in the dressing room.

pinch hitter

[cricket] – *a batsman promoted up the order with the job of scoring quick runs*

The term is fairly new to the game of cricket, only really gaining popular usage following the batting displays of Sri Lanka's Sanath Jayasuriya in the 1996 World Cup. Although he wasn't strictly promoted up the order as he had opened in One Day Internationals a number of times before, he took advantage of the early fielding restrictions by attacking the bowling right from the outset. This was a novel strategy at the time but his devastating success in the tournament of 79 from 76 balls against India, 44 from 27 against Kenya and then 82 from 44 against England in three successive games changed everyone's thinking about how to start an innings, and was seen a significant factor in ensuring Sri Lanka went on to become World Champions.

The term has been adopted by the cricketing fraternity from baseball, where it means a player substituted into the line-up because of injury or as a tactical replacement when a *hit* is needed. In other words, when it's an emergency and the team is *in a pinch*, it needs a *pinch hitter* to get it out of trouble.

pits

[motor racing] – *the area next to the track where teams service the cars*

Motor racing began almost immediately after the successful construction of the first petrol-fuelled cars, with the inaugural Paris to Rouen race in 1894. The following year saw the formation of the first motor racing club and America also held its first race. As the sport grew, racing cars developed and as the speeds increased, so did the need for greater maintenance – take the winning Mercedes in the French **Grand Prix** in 1908, for example, which shredded ten tyres on its way to victory! So in the same year, the Targa Florio – an open road endurance race held near Palermo in Sicily – saw the introduction of *pits*. These were shallow trenches dug next to the track to allow the mechanics to replace the detachable tyre rims in use at the time.

Pits have developed significantly since then and, among the banks of monitors and computer equipment, regularly see pit crews refuel a car and change all four wheels in less than seven seconds!

pole position

[motor racing] – *the number one slot on the starting grid*

Pole position is the optimal place to start a race from. Not only is it nearer the start line than any other car, it's also positioned so that the driver can take the first corner on the inside, and consequently shorter, line of the track. The term comes from horse-racing in the mid-19th century, when, if a horse 'had the pole', it had drawn the starting position nearest the post that denoted the starting line, on the inside boundary rails. It was adopted by the motor racing community in the 1950s.

Pompey

[football] – *a nickname for Portsmouth FC*

Portsmouth FC was founded in 1898 and shares its nickname with the city. Although the exact origin of the moniker is unclear, it is almost certainly of naval extraction and a number of theories abound. The simple thought is that all the pomp and ceremony synonymous with the Royal Navy and therefore on display in Portsmouth over the centuries became known as *pompey*, before being adopted by the city.

Some think that it lies in the fact that ships entering Portsmouth harbour enter *Pom. P.* in the ship's log as a reference to Portsmouth Point. Navigational charts also use this abbreviation.

Others believe that it derives from the 80-gun French warship *La Pompée* which was captured in 1793 before going on to fight with distinction as

HMS *Pompee* in the Battle of Algeciras Bay in 1801. It subsequently became the guardship of Portsmouth harbour in the early 19th century, before being broken up in 1817.

Perhaps apocryphal, but it is also said that one day when the naval temperance activist Dame Agnes Weston was delivering a lecture about the murder of the Roman general Pompey, a drunk sailor in the audience woke from a beery slumber and shouted 'Poor old Pompey!' before falling back to sleep.

In 1781, some sailors from Portsmouth also climbed Pompey's Pillar, the tallest ancient monument in Alexandria. One hundred feet above Egypt they toasted their achievement with punch and subsequently became known as the *Pompey Boys*.

So although I can't be sure how Portsmouth got their nickname, I do know that I always enjoyed the chant behind my goal whenever I played at Fratton Park: 'Play up Pompey, Play up Pompey!'

pool

[pool] – *a form of billiards played with balls and a cue on a baize-covered table with six pockets*

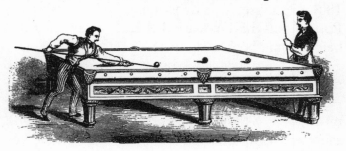

Billiards, originally played with three balls, was principally a two-player contest until the beginning of the 19th century. At this time, the British added more balls and created two other types of game to allow room for more players. *Pyramids* was played with fifteen unnumbered red balls. Another multi-player game used a variable number of coloured and spotted balls in a form of ante betting that gave it its name of *pool*. Each player would put in a stake and the winner of the game would scoop the pool of cash. The game is thought to have gained its name in Britain by 1820, and reached France by 1923, when rules posters for *jeu de la poule* began to appear.

Poppadom fingers

[cricket] – *a nickname for former England captain, Nasser Hussain*

As Madras-born Nasser Hussain was sidelined with amazing regularity throughout his career with a broken finger or thumb, his Essex and subsequently England teammates began to make light of the situation by likening his digits to *poppadoms*, the thin cracker typically served as an accompaniment to an Indian meal.

popping crease

[cricket] – *a line at each end of the pitch which a batsman must be behind to avoid being stumped or run out, and which a bowler must not overstep to avoid a no-ball being called*

The use of the term *crease* in cricket is in line with its basic meaning of *furrow*, two of which were originally cut in the pitch to mark out the necessary areas. This method was used until the introduction of painted white lines towards the end of the 19th century. The name *popping crease* comes from the very early days of the game. Before **stumps** (or their earlier predecessors) were introduced, there was a *popping hole* – a hole dug out of the pitch where the stumps now stand. Batsmen had to *pop* their bat in the hole on completion of a run and similarly, fielders had to *pop* the ball in it in order to run a batsman out (being bowled was not yet part of the game).

Posh

[football] – *the nickname for Peterborough United FC*

Although Peterborough United wasn't formed until 1934, the team's nickname was decided for them over a decade earlier. At the beginning of the 1920s the club's present-day London Road ground was home to a side called Fletton United. At the end of a very poor season in 1921, Fletton's player–manager Pat Tirrel set about rebuilding his side in an attempt to win the Northamptonshire League. He declared that he was looking for 'posh players for a posh new team'. Although the side would later disband, Peterborough United FC inherited the nickname on its formation in 1934, and it has remained with them ever since.

Postage Stamp

[golf] – *the 129-yard, **par**-3 8th hole at Royal Troon*

Originally this hole was called *Ailsa*, after Ailsa Craig, the prominent rock that emerges from the Atlantic off the Ayrshire coast and is clearly visible from the elevated tee (see ***fairy rock***). Although the shortest hole on any of the Open courses, it's far from the easiest, due to the tiny size of its green. In 1909, Willie Park Jr., a former Open Champion, described it in an article for *Golf Illustrated* as 'a pitching surface skimmed down to the size of a *postage stamp*', and the name stuck.

Because the green is surrounded by bunkers, the ball must reach it with the tee-shot. Tiger Woods found this out to his cost when he failed to find the green in the final round of the 1997 Open – shooting a triple-***bogey*** six as a result. At the Open in 1950, German Hermann Tissies took 15.

There have been successes there, of course, notably the hole-in-one by 71-year-old Gene Sarazen at the 1973 Open, 50 years after his appearance at Troon's inaugural Open in 1923. Despite this, it's still regarded by many as 'the hardest stamp in the world to lick'.

priest

[fishing] – *a small club with which game fish can be quickly and humanely dispatched after capture*

Traditionally a *priest* would pray for a dying man or woman on their deathbed to help ensure a safe passage to God. These implements take their name from the fact that similarly, although perhaps a little more harshly, they administer the 'last rites' to the fish.

There is often a *marrow spoon* on the other end of a priest. These take their name from the traditional slender table utensil with dished ends with which a diner could extract marrow from a bone during a meal. Once the priest has been used to kill the fish, the marrow spoon is then used to extract the contents from its stomach. By doing so, a fisherman can choose the most suitable fly to use to try and catch more fish in the same stretch of water.

professional's side

[golf] – *the high side of the hole*

It's common sense that a putt that breaks below the hole has no chance of going in, but that still doesn't seem to stop me hitting it there! However, professionals know better and although they still miss putts with a difficult break, you'll very rarely see it miss on the low side. Above the hole, they give themselves the best chance of the ball going in, and so us lowly amateurs talk in admiration of the *professional's side*.

puck

[ice hockey] – *a hard black
disc made of vulcanised rubber*

Although **hockey** had been played in Britain in
various guises for hundreds of years, it wasn't until
the 1820s that people began to play it on ice. The
idea was soon exported to the British protectorate
of Canada and gained considerable interest in the
second half of the 19th century. The certainty of
long cold winters in Canada soon saw ice hockey
become their national game. In the early years, a
rubber ball was used but proved unsatisfactory
because of the extreme bounce it generated on
the hard ice.

Around that time the Victoria Skating Rink
was built in Montreal. It was one of the world's
first indoor ice rinks. Before long however, its
owner had become fed up with the number of
windows being broken at his new venue by the
volatile rubber balls. By 3 March 1875 he couldn't

take it any more. On the sight of another breakage he stormed onto the ice with a knife, picked up the ball and cut it in half. The *puck*, albeit in need of a little modification, was born.

Though no one knows exactly how the puck got its name, some believe that it was chosen after the character in William Shakespeare's *A Midsummer Night's Dream*. Like the mischievous and irrepressible spirit, the puck moves frenziedly around the ice. However, it's more likely that it came from the verb *to puck* used in hurling for pushing or striking the ball – which in turn comes from the Gaelic word *puc* meaning to poke, punch or deliver a blow. Either way, many people these days simply call it the *biscuit*.

Pumas

[rugby union] – *the nickname of Argentina's national team*

When the side set off for South Africa in 1965, embarking on their first overseas tour, they were still without a nickname to rival the existing **Springboks** of their hosts. A reporter, trying to think of something suitable while following the tour, mistakenly took the jaguar on their team crest for a puma, and gave them the wrong name. Undeterred by the error, the press and the public continued to use the name before the team itself eventually adopted it. The crest of the *Pumas* still depicts a jaguar today.

Punch and Judy hitter

[baseball] – *a batter deemed to have little power*

The term was coined by former Los Angeles Dodgers manager Walter Emmons Alston who, when asked about a home run by San Francisco Giants slugger Willie 'Big Mac' McCovey, replied: 'When he belts a home run, he does it with such authority it seems like an act of God. You can't cry about it. He's not a *Punch and Judy* belter.'

pyjama cricket

[cricket] – *one-day cricket*

In 1977, Australian media mogul Kerry Packer and his Channel Nine network failed to win the television rights to cover Test matches and domestic cricket from the Australian Cricket Board. As a result, he set up a rival *World Series* by luring a number of high-profile players with very lucrative contracts. In order to also attract the necessary spectators, Packer introduced a number of innovations for the sport, such as night games with floodlights, coloured clothing, a white ball and black sightscreens. These concepts are still in use today for one-day cricket across the world, including the brightly-coloured team kits that give it the name *pyjama cricket*. The term is most commonly used in a derogatory context by purists of Test cricket who also sometimes refer to it as *hit and giggle*.

Queensberry Rules

[boxing] – *the set of rules commonly accepted in modern boxing*

Before this set of rules was put together by Arthur Graham Chambers and John Sholto Douglas in 1865 and introduced in 1867, boxing was on the whole a disorganised and brutal affair still fought with bare knuckles. The twelve different rules stipulated the use of a standard-sized 24-square-feet *ring*, three-minute rounds, a ten-second count, and the use of gloves for the first time. The rules take their name from Douglas, the 9th Marquess of *Queensberry*, who publicly endorsed them.

rabbit

[cricket] – *a poor batsman*

A *rabbit* is a batsman powerless to do anything when faced with the advancing bowler, similar to a rabbit caught in the headlights of an oncoming car. The term is sometimes also used to describe a particular batsman who is often dismissed by the same bowler. For example, Mike Atherton lost his wicket to Glenn McGrath nineteen times in his career – the most times any batsman has been dismissed by one bowler in international cricket history – earning him the label *Glenn McGrath's bunny*.

A *ferret* or *weasel* is an even worse batsman, based on them being sent in after a rabbit.

rabbit punch

[boxing] – *a punch to the back of the neck*

This is considered very dangerous because of the possible damage to the neck and spinal cord. As a result, it isn't allowed in boxing. It takes its name from the method used by hunters and farmers across the world to kill rabbits with a quick, hard strike to the back of the neck.

Rae's Creek

[golf] – *a creek that runs in front of the 12th green at the Augusta National Golf Club*

The creek also runs at the back of the 11th green and has a tributary near the tee at the 13th hole. It plays a very important role on the course, as the unfortunate American four-time *Masters* runner-up Tom Weiskopf found out to his cost at the tournament in 1980. On the 12th hole, he found the creek a record six times, shooting a 13 in the process.

The creek is connected to the Savannah River and named after John *Rae*, a well-known local who lived in the area in the 18th century. His house – the furthest up the Savannah River from Fort Augusta – was a much-needed safe haven for local residents during Indian attacks.

Rawalpindi Express

[cricket] – *a nickname for Pakistani cricketer Shoaib Akhtar*

Born on 13 August 1975 in Rawalpindi, Punjab, Shoaib Akhtar is the fastest recorded bowler the world has seen. So far, he's the first and only bowler to officially break the 100 mph barrier – achieving the milestone of 100.04 mph for the first time in a one-day international against New Zealand in 2002. Playing against England in the 2003 cricket World Cup, at 100.2 mph, he bowled the fastest official delivery ever unleashed by man.

real tennis

[real tennis] – *a game played with a racquet and ball in a court reminiscent of medieval cloisters, with either two or four players*

Initially known as *jeu de paume* (palm game), the game is thought to have been invented by French monks in monastery courtyards in the 11th or 12th century, and is widely considered as the predecessor of all modern racquet-and-ball games. In time, it became *tennis* – an adaptation of the word 'Tenez!' ('Take this!'), which the monks would shout at each other before serving the ball. The game quickly gained in popularity, and by the 15th century, the nobility in England and Scotland were modifying the courtyards of their houses into suitable playing areas.

It became known as *real tennis* only at the end of the 19th century, as a way of distinguishing it from the recently invented, but increasingly popular, *lawn tennis*.

red card

[football] – *the red-coloured card shown by a referee to a player to indicate that he is being dismissed from the pitch*

The concept of red and yellow cards for helping to officiate football matches was invented by English former referee and then chairman of the FIFA international referee committee, Kenneth George Aston. He was going about his business in the FIFA offices one day when a call came in from the 1966 World Cup tournament manager, querying whether Bobby and Jack Charlton had been cautioned in the England–Argentina match the previous day, in which the referee spoke only German. It turned out he'd just received a call from the Charlton brothers asking him to check – as the

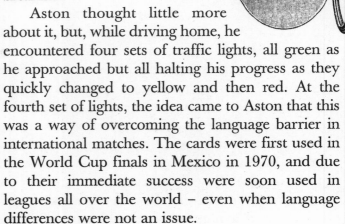

first they knew of
their booking was
from reading the
Sunday papers over
breakfast.

Aston thought little more
about it, but, while driving home, he
encountered four sets of traffic lights, all green as
he approached but all halting his progress as they
quickly changed to yellow and then red. At the
fourth set of lights, the idea came to Aston that this
was a way of overcoming the language barrier in
international matches. The cards were first used in
the World Cup finals in Mexico in 1970, and due
to their immediate success were soon used in
leagues all over the world – even when language
differences were not an issue.

Red Devils

[football] – *the nickname for Manchester United FC*

The club was founded in 1878 by workers of the Lancashire and Yorkshire Railway Company. They named it *Newton Heath LYR* and the club was soon nicknamed the *Heathens*. In 1902, however, the club were declared bankrupt, which led to the formation of *Manchester United*. Following this, the team was simply known as the *Reds* or *United*.

In the early 1950s, United manager Sir Matt Busby assembled a young, exciting and brilliant team, which the media quickly labelled the *Busby Babes*. Two league titles followed in 1956 and 1957. I have a very affectionate connection to this team, as England World Cup winner Nobby Stiles and myself were both signed by United in 1957 at the height of the Busby Babes' heyday (Nobby went on to sign professional forms and had a great career at

Old Trafford, while my dad made me 'get a proper job first' before being happy that I play football for a living).

The quality and success of the team meant Busby had entered the club into the European Champions Cup each year from 1956. Tragically, in 1958, when the team were returning from a game abroad against Red Star Belgrade, their plane crashed while trying to take off at Munich airport. Seven players were killed and Busby was severely injured. Another member of the team, the great Duncan Edwards, died a fortnight later and a further two were sufficiently injured to never play again. Although Busby recovered to rebuild and manage the team again, the Busby Babes moniker was now wholly inappropriate and was dropped.

At the beginning of the 1960s, Salford Rugby Club toured France and because of their red shirts, became known as the *Red Devils*. Busby liked it, as he thought that opposing teams would find the name intimidating, and he adopted it for his own side. Devil logos soon made their way into match programmes and onto club scarves, and in 1970, the official club badge was redesigned to incorporate a devil holding a pitch-fork. Manchester United have been the Red Devils ever since.

retired shirt

[football] – *the removal of a former player's squad number as a way of recognising their quality and loyalty to the club*

The symbolic gesture of this honour is in return for a player giving a team *the shirt off his back*. Although the practice has long been established in major North American sports (see **Iron Horse**), it is a recent development in football following the widespread usage of squad numbers in the 1990s.

Of course each club is entitled to do as they please with their own squad numbers and sometimes special arrangements are made. Upon the great Paolo Maldini announcing his retirement from AC Milan – with whom he spent his entire career and won seven Serie A and five Champions League titles – the club announced that it would *retire* his number 3 shirt but keep it open for one of his sons should either of them make it through the club's youth set-up and into the senior team.

In some cases, such as the Cameroon midfielder Marc-Vivien Foé, who died of heart failure while playing in the semi-final of the 2003 Confederations Cup, a shirt is retired posthumously to honour the player. In his particular case, Manchester City, Lens and Lyon all retired Foé's shirt in recognition of his time at their clubs. The Cameroon national team also tried to retire his shirt but was prevented by FIFA.

right church, wrong pew

[darts] – *a term for hitting a double, but the wrong number*

In more recent times this phrase has perhaps been more commonly superseded by *right house, wrong bed* and *right road, wrong door.* But its origins lie in the days of a more God-fearing nation when references to religion were far more common.

Darts has always been inextricably linked with betting, right back to its very beginnings with the throwing of arrows by archers in the Middle Ages. The game has therefore seen a large number of wagers over the centuries that have risen beyond a competitor's means. With so much at stake, and especially when going for a double, which would suggest it was nearing the end of the game, it was common for a player to say a little prayer on the ***oche*** before each dart.

ring

[boxing] – *the square area in which a bout takes place*

In the sport's early days, before the introduction of *rings* as we know them today, a group of spectators would form a circle around a fight as it unfolded. Those standing at the front would hold a rope as a way of marking out a ring. As boxing was illegal in many places at this point, it also allowed the fight organiser to get away if the police appeared, with only the loss of a bit of rope.

By the time more organised bouts and square fighting areas were introduced in the 19th century, the word 'ring' was fully engrained in boxing terminology and continued to be used.

Road Hole

[golf] – *the 461-yard,* **par**-*4 17th hole on the Old Course, St Andrews*

This is considered by many to be the hardest par 4 in the world. It starts with a blind drive over where the old tram shed once stood, now an outbuilding of the Old Course Hotel. Players usually pick out a letter from the hotel logo on the building wall as their line, but must choose wisely as the fairway narrows to under ten paces. A little too left and you will be in knee-high fescue, a little too right and you are out of bounds in the hotel's pond. Up ahead, however, the hole's greatest dangers lie in wait. First, there's the notorious *Road* bunker, which sits beside the green. It has destroyed many golfers' rounds over the years, notably Tommy Nakajima's at the 1978 Open – he took four to get out, leading to a quintuple-**bogey** nine.

If you clear what many locals still refer to as the *Sands of Nakajima* but fail to stop the ball on the green, you will find yourself on or over the old gravel turnpike road from which the hole takes its name. Land on it and you have to play off it, so kiss goodbye to the sole of your wedge. Land over it and the chances are your ball will be tucked up against the stone wall behind it, affording you no backswing.

Despite its innocuous name, the *Road Hole* is anything but easy.

Rocket

[snooker] – *a nickname for Ronnie O'Sullivan*

Like Jimmy *'Whirlwind'* White before him and Alex *'Hurricane'* Higgins before that, Ronnie *'Rocket'* O'Sullivan, or the *Essex Exocet* as he's otherwise known, isn't slow around a snooker table. In the World Championship on 21 April 1997, he compiled the fastest maximum 147 break ever recorded. It took him five minutes and twenty seconds. That's an average of one shot every nine seconds.

Roland Garros

[tennis] – *the French Open*

Roland Garros was arguably the world's first real fighter pilot. After several missions in the First World War, he decided that flying and shooting was too difficult and so attached a forward-firing machine gun to his plane. The weapon despatched bullets through the rotating propeller to which he attached steel deflector plates for those that hit.

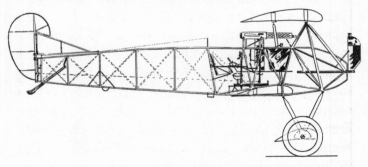

In March 1915, Garros shot down five German aircraft, an achievement that subsequently saw him dubbed an *ace* by an American newspaper. From that point on the term was attributed to any other Allied pilot that shot down five enemy planes while dogfighting.

The following month, however, he was shot down himself and forced to crash land behind German lines. He tried to burn his aircraft so as to protect the secret of his forward-firing machine gun, but was unsuccessful and was caught. He was placed in a German camp for the following three years until he escaped in February 1918 and promptly returned to service in France. On 5 October 1918, he was shot down again and killed near Vouziers, Ardennes, a month before the end of the war.

Nearly a decade later, in 1927, the celebrated French Davis Cup team, or Musketeers as they became known, pulled off one of the biggest shocks in 20th-century sport. They upset all the odds by winning the Cup on American soil, and in doing so, set up a rematch in 1928, in Paris. The occasion needed a stadium worthy of its stature and so the French Tennis Federation approached the Stade Français club for three hectares of land on which to build. Stade Français agreed, but only on the condition that the stadium be named after one of their most renowned former members – Monsieur Roland Garros. The venue has played host to the French Open ever since, and like Wimbledon, the tournament takes its official name from where it's played.

rope-a-dope

[boxing] – *a tactic whereby a fighter feigns being trapped on the ropes, encouraging his opponent to hit him and consequently tire himself out*

Muhammad Ali used this tactic to great effect on several occasions during his career, notably making a *dope* of the undefeated Heavyweight Champion, George Foreman in Zaire, in the 1974 fight billed the *Rumble in the Jungle*. Ali let Foreman, possibly the hardest-hitting heavyweight in boxing history, unleash on him for several rounds. Then, according to Foreman, Ali whispered 'Is that all you got, George?' before knocking him out in the eighth round.

Ali named this strategy as *rope-a-dope* while being interviewed in the mid-1970s, long after he had employed it for the first time.

ruck

[rugby union] – *a phase of play where one or more players from each team, who are on their feet, in physical contact, close around the ball on the ground*

In Medieval Scandinavia, the word *ruke* was used to describe a *pile* or *heap*, usually of hay or fuel of some sort. The English adopted the word and over time it became *ruck*. It also acquired a selection of new meanings, its most common usage being to describe a large number or group of undistinguished people or things – very similar to a modern-day ruck in rugby in many ways. Although there are many rules governing the ruck, it sometimes just degenerates into a mass or throng of writhing bodies, not unlike the mass fights organised between rival villages in the Middle Ages.

rugby

[rugby union] – *a sport played with an oval ball, H-shaped goals and two teams of fifteen players*

The popular view is that the sport was born in 1823 when a pupil at *Rugby* School in Warwickshire called William Webb Ellis picked up the ball and ran with it while playing football. Although historians dispute the accuracy of this legend, there is no doubt that the sport *did* develop at around that time at the English public school from which it takes its name. The first ever rugby club was then formed in 1843 at Guy's Hospital, London, and the sport's first rules published by Rugby School in 1845.

Ruthian

[baseball] – *an adjective used to describe a particularly long hit*

Babe Ruth hit 714 home runs in his career, many travelling over 500 feet, earning him an assortment of nicknames, including the *Great Bambino*, the *Sultan of Swat* and the *Colossus of Clout*. On 18 July 1921 (the year that he hit at least one 500-foot home run in all eight American League cities), Ruth hit the ball out of Detroit's Navin Field stadium. It landed on the far side of the street, just under 600 feet away – verifiably the longest home run in the history of Major League Baseball. His consistent long-distance hitting saw the emergence of the adjective *Ruthian*, a term players still aspire to today.

The 46-ounce Louisville Slugger solid ash bat with which he hit the first ever home run at the new Yankee Stadium (or *The House that Ruth Built* as it quickly became known) on 18 April 1923, sold at Sotheby's in 2004 for a Ruthian US$1.26 million.

Ryder Cup

[golf] – *a team event contested biennially by Europe and the USA*

Officially called the Ryder Cup Matches, the event and its trophy take their name from Samuel A. *Ryder*, a wealthy Englishman from St Albans in Hertfordshire, who had made his fortune selling penny seed packets to English gardeners. In 1926, after having watched an unofficial match between British and American teams at Wentworth, Ryder had a drink with some of the players including Walter Hagan and Abe

Mitchell. During the evening it was suggested that the fixture should be established on a more regular and official basis, so Ryder immediately pledged to donate a cup, and to 'give £5 to each of the winning players, and give a party afterwards, with champagne and chicken sandwiches!'

True to his word, Ryder commissioned Mappin & Webb to make a solid gold trophy to the value of £250. The first official Ryder Cup Matches was arranged for 1927 and the event and trophy which bear his name have been contested ever since.

In spite of a few changes to the format of the event over the years – the main amendment being the expansion of the British team to include Ireland and then all of Europe – there can be few men that have left such a fantastic legacy for a sport.

Sarazen Bridge

[golf] – *a stone footbridge that crosses over the water hazard in front of the green on the par-5 15th hole at the Augusta National Course*

The following words are written on a plaque at the bridge:

ERECTED TO COMMEMORATE THE
TWENTIETH ANNIVERSARY OF THE FAMOUS
'DOUBLE EAGLE' SCORED BY GENE SARAZEN
ON THIS HOLE, APRIL 7, 1935, WHICH GAINED
HIM A TIE FOR FIRST PLACE WITH CRAIG
WOOD AND IN THE PLAY-OFF WON THE
SECOND MASTERS TOURNAMENT.

DEDICATED APRIL 6, 1955

See **Shot heard round the world.**

scorpion kick

[football] – *a peculiar move where a player jumps forward, places their hands on the ground and then kicks the ball away with their heels*

This term was given to an outrageous skill invented and perfected by Colombian goalkeeper René Higuita. Instead of catching a high incoming ball, he would allow it to go over his head, bringing both legs and feet upwards to make contact with the ball behind his back, producing a scorpion-like movement. The degree of difficulty is such that the technique is not just dangerous for any keeper, it's misguided. However it is, naturally, highly entertaining and when Higuita did do it, he rarely got it wrong. I actually noticed him practising the move during the pre-match warm-up before the England vs. Colombia international at Wembley in 1995, when he famously used it on a goal-bound ball from Jamie Redknapp to the delight and admiration of the predominantly English crowd. 'I call it my scorpion kick and I try to do it whenever possible', he explained afterwards.

scrum

[rugby union] – *a way of restarting the game whereby the two sets of forwards bind together to form a closed huddle with a central aisle – each set then tries to push the opposing team off the ball when it is put in by the scrum-half*

The term *scrum* is an abbreviation of *scrummage*, which in turn is a modification of the no-longer used *scrimmage*. The word *scrimmage* is thought to derive from *skirmish*: a brief battle between small groups, usually part of a longer or larger battle or war.

Scuderia

[motor racing] – *the Ferrari Formula One team*

Scuderia Ferrari is Italian for *Ferrari Stable*, which is often liberally translated as *Team Ferrari*. It's the name for the *Gestione Sportiva*, the division of the Ferrari automobile company concerned with racing. It was founded by Enzo Ferrari in 1929 as a sponsor for amateur drivers, racing mostly in Alfa Romeos until the production of the first true Ferrari car a decade later. The team then made its debut in Formula One a decade after that.

So although *Scuderia* literally means just *Stable*, it has become synonymous with Ferrari over the last half a century as the team has achieved unparalleled success in the sport.

The legions of passionate followers of the Scuderia are known as the *tifosi* – Italian for *fans*. A single fan is a *tifoso*, and a female fan is a *tifosa*.

Shot heard round the world

[miscellaneous] – *a phrase used to describe a number of dramatic moments in sports history*

In the final round of the 1935 **Masters** at Augusta, the legendary Gene Sarazen hit a 225-yard 4-wood on his second shot at the *par*-5 15th. It went in, and his **albatross** secured him a place in a play-off, which he won.

In 1951, the Brooklyn Dodgers and New York Giants finished level at the top of the National League and played a three-game play-off to decide the Championship. In the deciding game, trailing 4-2 with two men on base and a man out in the bottom of the ninth inning, Giants' Bobby

Thompson hit a home run, allowing himself and the two base runners to score, securing his team the title.

In 1976, in the Pheonix-Boston basketball championship series, Garfield Heard successfully fired an arcing turnaround jump shot over twenty feet to send the game into a third overtime.

In 1989, Paul Caligiuri curled a 35-yard strike over the Trinidad and Tobago goalkeeper and into the net, securing the USA a place in their first World Cup for 40 years.

The term often used to describe these moments originates from *Concord Hymn*, the classic poem written by American Ralph Waldo Emerson in 1837. In it he describes the impact of the battle of Old North Bridge on the first day of the American War of Independence:

By the rude bridge that arched the flood,
Their flag to April's breeze unfurled;
Here once the embattled farmers stood;
And fired a shot heard round the world.

show the bowler the maker's name

[cricket] – *to bat defensively with a straight bat*

Coaches traditionally shout this at batsmen while they practise in the nets. The best way to *show the bowler the maker's name* is to get on the front foot and point the face of the bat, where the manufacturer's logo usually is, straight back down the pitch at the bowler so he can read it. Doing this encourages the use of a straight bat, producing the most effective defensive shot available in the game.

What remains to be seen, however, is if this expression will survive the current transition in the modern game – whereby bats are used to advertise

anything and everything, and the maker's name is often removed in order to make space for a more lucrative sponsor. Before the International Cricket Council relaxed the rules on this, only the bat manufacturer or the batsmen themselves were meant to display logos on the bat. This led to the practice of large companies buying little bat factories and then producing a handful of bats a year, which meant they could send out batsmen to the middle wielding portable billboards.

silly point

[cricket] – *a fielding position very close to the batsman, square on the off-side*

As the name suggests, this is not a great place to be put by your captain. In the early days of cricket this position was known as *point of the bat* or *bat's end*. Over time, as it dawned on cricketers that standing so close to the bat as it was being swung was a peculiar thing to do, it became *silly point*; the fielder has to be silly to agree to stand there.

skipping

[golf] – *the annual tradition during the practice rounds for the **Masters** whereby players try to reach the green at the 170-yard **par**-3 16th by hitting their ball along the surface of the pond from the tee*

Although it's cheating a little, the best approach – so I'm told – is to take your shot from the downslope of the bank just in front of the tee. That way, if you hit it at the right strength, the downslope creates the necessary spin to make the ball *skip* across the water. From that spot, and at that angle, five or six *skips* should see your ball onto the green. Any fewer and you haven't hit your ball hard enough and it will lose momentum and disappear into the pond.

It's worth knowing because if you skip the *skipping* as it were on a practice round in Masters week, you'll incite the wrath of the Augusta crowd. To avoid the boos, most try it in their own particular way. 'I toe in a long iron and try to hit a low hook that skips about six times', revealed three-time Major winner Nick Price. 'That takes talent. Vijay can do it. He probably practises it – he practises everything else', he says with admiration.

Augusta's least official tradition began with the great Lee Trevino. He can't remember which year it was but he performed it in the tournament itself. 'I hadn't played well and was off early Sunday', recounted Trevino. 'It had rained a lot overnight, and the water on 16 was up to the bank. That water was perfect, like glass. I said, "Beautiful." I was about eight over par. That baby took three skips and ran up in the middle of the green, and I two-putted for par.'

slam-dunk smash

[tennis] – *a smash hit high and early by a jumping player in mid-air*

This takes its name from both the standard overhead *smash*, a move that has been used in tennis since it began, and the basketball term *slam dunk*, whereby a player jumps in the air and powerfully and dramatically *dunks* the ball through the basket from close range to score, grabbing onto the hoop with both hands. In tennis, *slam-dunk smash* was coined for the move frequently employed and made famous in the 1990s by the record fourteen-time **Grand Slam** winner, Pete Sampras.

sledging

[cricket] – *barracking of the batsmen by the fielding side in order to disturb their concentration*

The Australians are known to be some of the most prolific and effective *sledgers* in the game, and so it's fitting that the term originates from their country. It's thought that in the 1960s, a fast bowler from New South Wales called Graham Corling made an awful faux pas at a party in front of mixed company. Someone promptly told him that he was 'as subtle as a sledgehammer'. Apparently, this was then abbreviated to *sledgehammer*, and then *sledge*. A further connection was made to the song 'When a Man Loves a Woman', by Percy Sledge, and Corling acquired the nickname *Percy*.

Although the practice of verbally abusing batsmen has been around since cricket began, it was becoming more widespread at the beginning of the 1970s, and so those familiar with the story called it sledging.

In spite of their sledging prowess, the Australians have also been the victims of some great retorts over the years. Take Jimmy Ormond's Ashes exchange with Mark Waugh. The Australian asked Ormond what a man of his lowly cricketing stature was doing out in the middle. 'I may not be the best cricketer in the world', responded Ormond, 'but at least I'm the best cricketer in my family'.

Or there was Zimbabwean Eddo Brandes' discussion with Glenn McGrath, after Brandes had played and missed at another McGrath delivery. 'Oi, Brandes, why are you so f**ing fat?' enquired McGrath. 'Because every time I f**k your wife, she gives me a biscuit', he replied. Even the Australians were in hysterics.

slider

[cricket] – *a straight delivery by a wrist-spin bowler which is released from the front of the hand and deliberately floated to a full length. It then bounces less than the batsman might expect because of the backspin imparted on the ball*

It's a fairly common misconception that this delivery was invented by Shane Warne, when actually it has had several successful exponents over the years. The Australian leg-spinner Peter Philpott was using it in the 1960s, the great Richie Benaud before that and then another Australian, Doug Ring, before that. The confusion lies in the name.

After the ***Lord's*** Test in 1953, in which Benaud's bowling had been comfortably dealt with by Trevor Bailey and Willie Watson before Ring got them both out, the touring Australian side set off for Bristol by train. On the journey, Ring took an apple from the fruit bowl and used it to demonstrate the grip of his invention to Benaud, who before long would refer to it as his *sliding top-spinner*. Although much the same ball, Philpott would later call it an *orthodox backspinner*. It wasn't until Warne began to use it in such a destructive fashion three decades later that Richie Benaud, having become probably the best cricket sage and TV pundit in the world, would simply refer to it on air as the *slider*.

Slow Death

[cricket] – *a nickname for Jamaican umpire Steve Bucknor*

Stephen Anthony Bucknor is widely regarded as one the best umpires in the world. He has umpired more Test matches than anyone else in the history of the game. Nevertheless, it hasn't speeded up his decision-making while out in the middle over the years. 'I have never been hasty to make decisions', admits Bucknor. 'By nature, I like to take my time to do things. Patience is a virtue for me' – a comment that will resonate with thousands of batsmen the world over who have been made to wait in terror as he takes his lengthy trade-mark pause for thought while deciding whether or not to raise the finger of doom. If you see the characteristic nod, then you know you are about to be a victim of the *Slow Death*.

snooker

[snooker] – *a game played with fifteen red and six other coloured balls and a cue on a baize-covered table with pockets*

Although billiards dates back to the beginning of the 15th century, this game was invented much later in 1875 – when some British Army officers of a Devonshire regiment and their Colonel, Sir Neville Chamberlain (no relation of the later Prime Minister) were bored at their Mess while posted in Jubbulpore, India. Soon after, a young subaltern arrived at the regiment, bringing the term *snooker* – used for new recruits at the Royal Military Academy where he had trained. Later, while playing the as-yet-unnamed game, an officer missed an easy pot, prompting Chamberlain to call him a snooker. Both the game and its new name were spread across the British Empire by the movement of the military that played it.

soccer

[football] – *a name for **football** that is predominantly used in the US, among other countries*

The Football Association was formed in London in 1863 from a meeting of eleven clubs and schools to establish the laws of the game. One of the rules distinctly prohibited the carrying of the ball, and the sport required a name to distinguish it from **rugby** football, so *Association Football* was chosen. But on the whole, people found this long-winded and abbreviated it to *socca*. It was then adapted to *socker*, before *soccer* was finally settled on by the end of the 19th century. It's thought to have evolved with public school and University students, most notably from Oxford, thanks to their propensity to shorten words and then add *-er*. Rugby was also afforded a similar treatment at the time, becoming *rugger*.

I'm glad to say it's rarely used in this country any more, as I prefer the more self-explanatory *football*. Soccer was, however, also adopted by the US, and they still use the name as a way of differentiating the sport from both rugby and, more importantly for them, the sport of American football.

southpaw

[boxing] – *a left-hander, and therefore a boxer who leads with his right hand*

In America, as the game of baseball evolved, people realised that ballparks should be designed so that the more common right-handed batter would face east in order to avoid the late afternoon or early evening sun shining in his eyes. This meant that the pitcher would face west, but if he was left-handed, he would be throwing with his south-side hand, or *southpaw*. In time, the term came to represent left-handers in sport in general, and it was adopted by American boxing before making its way across the Atlantic to Britain in the mid-19th century.

The Australian equivalent is a *mollydooker*.

spaghetti-legs routine

[football] – *a goalkeeper's trick employed to distract a penalty taker*

Some goalkeepers pride themselves on their ability to out-psych a penalty taker. However, they usually try and achieve it a little more subtly than Liverpool's Bruce Grobbelaar did at the penalty shoot-out of the European Cup Final vs. AS Roma in 1984.

Played in the Olympic Stadium in Rome, the partisan crowd went wild when Steve Nicol missed Liverpool's first penalty, but after Agostino Di Bartolomei and Phil Neal had made it 1-1, Bruno Conti missed to even things up. Graeme Souness, Ubaldo Righetti and Ian Rush were all successful before Francesco Graziani stepped up to take his. As Grobbelaar walked over to take his place in goal, his legs began to wobble dramatically in mock fear of the ensuing kick. Whether Grobbelaar's antics put Graziani off will never be known but the Italian sent his spot-kick sailing over the bar and Liverpool won their fourth European Cup.

Afterwards, Grobbelaar called it his *spaghetti-legs routine*. 'People said I was being disrespectful to

their players, but I was just testing their concentration under pressure. I guess they failed that test.'
In the Champions League Final 21 years later, another Italian side would fail the same test put to them by another Liverpool goalkeeper. Inspired by Grobbelaar's antics of the past, Jerzy Dudek replicated the routine and saved penalties from both Andrea Pirlo and Andriy Shevchenko to ensure the top European trophy returned to Anfield for the first time since 1984.

Having fought in a civil war in Zimbabwe, Grobbelaar could appreciate that football was not as important as some people would suggest. Nevertheless, he enjoyed thirteen successful seasons at Anfield, becoming the most decorated goalkeeper in league history. Then, in 1994, having moved on to Southampton, he was charged with match fixing during his time at Liverpool. I studied the games in question and had no hesitation in speaking on his behalf as an expert witness at three trials, which ended in his being found not guilty.

He believed that the match-fixing scandal arose because the press didn't like the person they perceived as arrogant and had a reputation for clowning around in games. 'Goalkeepers aren't supposed to do that', he reflected.

Spireites

[football] – *the nickname for Chesterfield FC*

The fourth oldest football club in England takes its name from the bizarre spire of the town's 14th-century Parish Church of St Mary and All Saints. It rises to a height of 228 feet above the ground and leans perilously almost 10 feet to the south-west. What's more, from base to pinnacle it twists anticlockwise through more than 45°, and is still moving. The spire also just sits on top of the stone tower, balancing with no apparent fixing. How it remains standing I'm not quite sure.

Built in 1362, it remained straight for several centuries before it began to twist. There are several theories for the movements that have emerged over time. Some think that unseasoned or green timber was used; this was fairly common practice in the Middle Ages as it was less wearing on the tools of the time. Having said that, if green timber was used it was usually for less ambitious or permanent constructions than a 228-foot-high church spire! It's also thought that there may have been a shortage of skilled craftsmen at the time, after the Black Death had taken its toll on the area. Folklore also talks of two imps that were sent by Satan to do his evil work. Their first act was to twist the spire of Chesterfield Parish Church before heading off to wreak more havoc across the region (see *Imps*).

I have huge affection for the crooked spire. It was at this church in my hometown that I began a relationship with a girl called Margaret Miles which continues to this day, albeit as Mrs or Megs Wilson!

Springboks

[rugby union] – *the nickname for the South African National Team*

In 1906, the South African national rugby union team toured Britain for the first time. During the tour, concerned that the British press were going to coin an annoying nickname for their side, the team manager, tour staff and team captain Paul Roos, got together for an impromptu meeting in order to come up with their own. Afterwards, Roos informed journalists that they were to be called *De Springbokken*. The *Daily Mail* duly obliged and immediately ran an article referring to the team as the *Springboks*. The team had a springbok badge placed on the left breast pocket of their blazers and the name has remained with them ever since.

Spurs

[football] – *a nickname for Tottenham Hotspur FC*

In 1882, boys from Haringey's Hotspur cricket club and the St John's Presbyterian local grammar school got together and decided to form a football club. Reputedly in a meeting under a street lamp on Tottenham High Street, close to the current ground, they decided to retain the cricket club name and simply call it Hotspur FC.

The cricketers among them had initially chosen the name Hotspur after the 14th century's Sir Henry Percy, or *Harry Hotspur* as he was otherwise known – the eldest son of the 1st Earl of Northumberland. By the 19th century, the Northumberland dynasty had significant ties with Haringey, owning large tracts of land in the area. Harry Hotspur was a great warrior and had acquired his new name as a result of the large riding spurs on his armour and fiery devil-may-care bravery in battle against the Scots towards the end of the 14th century. In 1403 he led a rebellion against Henry IV but was killed in the Battle of Shrewsbury when hit in the mouth with an arrow. Something that your average Tottenham fan will forget to tell you at this point is that after his death Henry IV had his body quartered and sent to different corners of England and his head stuck on a pole at York's gates. However, his bravery and fiery temperament were later immortalised in William Shakepseare's Henry IV, Part I. Ironically, as a seventeen-year-old boy I played the part of Hotspur in our school play!

Throughout 1883, Hotspur FC were playing their matches on Tottenham marshes but it soon became apparent that they had to distinguish themselves from another team in the area going by the name of London Hotspur. So in 1884, they renamed themselves Tottenham Hotspur Football and Athletic Club, but before long, like the large, sharp spiked wheels on the heels of their hero's armour, they were simply known as the *Spurs*.

squash

[squash] – *a racquet-and-ball sport played by two or four people on a court surrounded by four walls*

Although there had been many racquet-and-ball games in existence in Britain since the Middle Ages, *squash* was not invented until much more recently. At the beginning of the 19th century, bored inmates of Fleet Prison on London's South Bank invented the game of *racquets* while spending their days hitting balls against the walls of their cells with makeshift racquets. Strangely enough, the game was then picked up by Harrow School on the other side of London, around 1820. About ten years later, some pupils were playing racquets when the ball they were playing with punctured. In spite of this, they continued to play, discovering that as the ball *squashed* on impact with the wall, it created a very different game. Their invention proved popular among pupils and staff alike, and the first four squash courts were built at the school in 1864.

Stableford

[golf] – *a type of competition in which the scoring system is based on a player's handicap and the stroke index of each hole*

You get one point for a net *bogey*, two points for a net *par*, three points for a net *birdie*, four points for a net *eagle* and five for a net *albatross*. Add all your points up at the end and the player with the most wins. Simple! And so thought Dr Frank Barney Gorton *Stableford* when he invented the system at Wallasey Golf Club in 1931.

Before serving as a major in the Great War, Stableford had had a handicap of plus one, but by the time he returned his handicap had slipped to 8. This, coupled with Wallasey's notoriously strong winds, meant he found it almost impossible to reach the greens of the long par-4s in two, which infuriated him enormously, until he devised the system still used by many club golfers today: 'I was practising on the second fairway at Wallasey Golf Club one day in the latter part of 1931 when the thought ran through my mind that many players in competitions got very little fun since they tore up their cards after playing only a few holes, and I wondered if anything could be done about it.' Wallasey held the first Stableford competition on 16 May 1932.

steeplechase

[horse racing] – *a race of between two and four-and-a-half miles in length, over fences that are a minimum of four-and-a-half feet high*

In Ireland in 1752, 'a certain Mr Callaghan and his friend, Mr Edmund Blake, made a sporting wager to race cross country from Buttevant Church to the steeple of Saint Leger Church, a distance of roughly four-and-a-half miles'. This extract from a document found in the library of Dromoland Castle is believed to be an account of the birth of the *steeplechase* – a race in which orientation of the course was originally by churches and their steeples. This usually entailed negotiating whatever obstacles the countryside had to offer and, although this notion of diverse fences and ditches remains, the orientation by church does not. In spite of this, races such as the Grand National are still known as *steeplechases*.

sticky dog

[cricket] – *a wet pitch drying in the sun*

When a pitch has been rained on, it becomes soft and *sticky*, making it a *dog* to bat on. *Sticky dogs* are no longer a feature of top-flight cricket, as pitches are covered immediately when it begins to rain – but in the past, they were very much a part of the game. A drying wicket would lend itself perfectly to certain bowlers, notably England's Derek Underwood, who gained the nickname of *Deadly* for the havoc he could wreak in such situations. The **Ashes** series of 1968 saw England go to the last Test at the **Oval** one-nil down. Nevertheless, they dictated the final match and looked set for victory on the last session of the series when a violent thunderstorm seemed to bring Australian salvation. The game finally resumed, giving England one last gasp at squaring the series. Underwood proceeded to take four wickets in 27 balls – securing victory with five minutes to spare and bringing about one of the most dramatic conclusions to a Test in cricketing history.

stumps

[cricket] – *the three wooden sticks which the batsman must protect from the bowling*

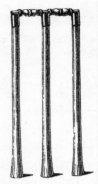

When cricket was first played in the 13th century, its early practitioners used the cleared forests of Southern England as playing areas. Tree *stumps* that remained in the ground were used as the bowler's target.

Stumps have progressed somewhat since then, seeing the introduction of built-in cameras in the early 1990s and, more recently, stump microphones. Some players see these microphones as a regression, however, as they hinder their ability to *sledge* opposing batsmen while out in the middle. That didn't stop Australian wicketkeeper Ian Healy from the act – when stockily-built Sri Lankan Arjuna Ranatunga asked for a runner during a one-day international, Healy was picked up on the mic suggesting that 'You don't get a runner for being an overweight, unfit, fat, f**k.'

stymie

[golf] – *a situation in which the path to the flag is blocked*

This term is now applied to any shot when there is something obstructing your intended route to the target, but it comes more specifically from a rule that was abolished in 1951. Nowadays, if an opponent's ball blocks your path on the green you can ask them to mark it. But before then, if their ball blocked your path you were *stymied*; it was tough luck – you had to play into it, over it or around it. The one exception was if the two balls were less than six inches apart, in which case the non-striker would lift their ball and replace it once the striker had putted. This is why many scorecards at that time measured six inches across.

Stymies used to play a significant role in the outcome of many matches, notably the final round of the Amateur Championship at St Andrews in 1930. On the first extra hole in a play-off with Cyril Tolley, the great Bobby Jones left his ***birdie*** putt a couple of inches from the cup in the line of his opponent's ball. It was the perfect *stymie* and secured him victory. Later that year, he went on to win the Open Championship, the US Open, and the US Amateur Championship, completing the original ***Grand Slam*** – this phenomenal achievement all started with a stymie!

The word itself derives from the Old Scottish vernacular for a person with little spiritual belief, or someone who has difficulty 'seeing the light', similarly to a stymied golfer who has difficulty seeing the hole.

Sugar

[boxing] – *a nickname for – pound-for-pound – the best boxer of all time*

Walker Smith Jr. was born in Ailey, Georgia, on 3 May 1921. He began boxing soon after moving to New York, aged twelve. He tried to enter his first boxing tournament at fourteen but was turned away as he didn't have the necessary Amateur Athletic Union boxing card to prove he was sixteen. So he borrowed one from his friend, Ray Robinson, and went on to win the New York Golden Gloves Championship under that name. Upon seeing the young boxer fight for the first time, his future coach George Gainford exclaimed that his style was 'sweet as *sugar*'. Walter Smith Jr. had become *Sugar* Ray Robinson, and by the time he retired at the age of 44, he hadn't been knocked out once.

sweeper

[football] – *a player who roams behind the defenders without specific man-marking duties*

The idea of this position is that the player will *sweep up* any problems that should arise if the line of orthodox defenders is breached. Because of the fluidity of the *sweeper*'s role in comparison with other defenders, the position is also referred to as the *libero*, the Italian word for *free*. Finding a player clever enough to maximise this role is the key. I always admired the great two-time European Footballer of the Year Franz Beckenbauer's ability to clear up at the back, but also to break forward and truly maximise the free role. His command of the ball and play was unrivalled in that position at the time, and so saw him affectionately nicknamed *Emperor Franz* and *The Kaiser*.

sweet science

[boxing] – *the art or practice of boxing*

Over a century before the introduction of the **Queensberry Rules** and the consequent coordination of boxing as a whole, the British champion of the time, Jack Broughton, had formulated the sport's first code in the form of the *London Prize Ring Rules*. Motivated by the untimely death of one of his opponents during a bout in 1743, he created the regulations in the hope of turning boxing into a more definite science. A little later, in 1818, English writer Pierce Egan referred to the sport as 'the *sweet science* of bruising' in *Boxiana; or Sketches of Modern Pugilism*, his collection of boxing articles. The term was finally adopted and popularised by sportswriters around the mid-20th century, notably by the much admired American journalist A.J. Liebling – who named his own first collection of boxing articles *The Sweet Science* in Egan's honour.

Texas wedge

[golf] – *a name for the putter when it's used to putt from off the green*

The term originated in the 1940s on the golf courses of Texas, USA, before being popularised by the great Ben Hogan. Without the high-tech irrigation systems that golf courses enjoy today, they used to rely on rain for their water. In the more arid parts of Texas this would often lead to very dry and hard fairways. As a result, players would often land their ball short in the hope that it would bounce up onto the green. This tactic would often see players drop it too short, with the ball coming to a stop before the green. In order to deal with the extremely hard fairway and very short grass, players would then often decide it best to pull out their *Texas wedge* so as to minimise the risk of their next shot.

Three Finger Brown

[baseball] – *a nickname for baseball legend, Mordecai Brown*

When feeding material into the corn-shredder on the farm aged seven, Mordecai Brown slipped and the machine removed much of his index finger while badly damaging the others. Doctors did their best to repair his hand but it was in a real mess. To make matters worse, while chasing a pig a few weeks later, he fell and broke several of the remaining finger bones in the same hand. Embarrassed by his second clumsy accident, he kept it quiet and so the bones were never reset. In time, they reformed, but in the most peculiar shape.

As Brown grew up, he worked in the Western Indiana coal mines, playing third base for the company baseball team at the weekends. Then in 1898, when Brown was 22, an injury to the team's pitcher forced Brown to the mound as an emergency replacement. It soon became apparent that the manner in which he had to grip the ball resulted in an abnormal amount of spin. He went on to become one of the best Major League Baseball pitchers of his era, and in the newspaper headlines, became *Three Finger Brown*.

tiger line

[golf] – *the most direct, and hence risky, line for a drive or approach shot*

The back or competition tee is often described as a *tiger tee*. Contrary to popular belief, this has nothing to do with Mr Woods. According to Peter Alliss, it comes from Sand Moor Golf Club in Leeds where model tigers were used to denote the back tees.

Similarly, the term *tiger line* has been in use since long before Woods was even born. In 1959, Ian Fleming described in his book *Goldfinger* the par-4 2nd hole at Royal St George's, Sandwich, as a 'three hundred and seventy yard dogleg to the left with deep cross-bunkers daring you to take the tiger's line' – meaning rather than go around the deep rough, go straight over it on the same line as a tiger would go through it.

This is why rough, bushes or trees on a golf course are also sometimes referred to as *jungle* or *tiger country*.

Timeless Test

[cricket] – *the final Test in the 1938–39 series between South Africa and England*

This match unsurprisingly brought the era of play-to-the-finish Tests to a close. It saw an aggregate of 1,981 runs scored over a period of ten days, 43 hours and sixteen minutes of playing time, yet still failed to produce a winner! After more than a week, England were finally set 696 to win in their second innings but on the tenth day, only 42 runs short and with five wickets still in hand, they were forced to abandon the game. It had gone on so long that they had to make a dash straight from the ground to their boat which had finally given up waiting and was about to set sail for England without them. The match was ruled a draw and would forever be known as the *Timeless Test*.

Toffeemen

[football] – *the nickname for Everton FC*

The *Toffeemen* or *Toffees* have been the established nicknames for the club from its very early days and are likely to have come about as a result of the following story. Many early club meetings were held at the Queen's Head Hotel, which was near Ye Anciente Everton Toffee House run by a woman known as Old Ma Bushell. She produced *Everton Toffees*, which she sold in large numbers to the fans that came to watch Everton play in the new Football League. However, in 1892, the club moved from Anfield to Goodison Park, displacing her market and consequently reducing her sales to nothing.

Instead, near the new ground was Mother Noblett's Toffee Shop, but Mother Noblett couldn't take advantage of her new-found bit of fortune, as Old Ma Bushell had patented the Everton Toffee. So Mother Noblett created the Everton Mint, which – with the black and white stripes of an earlier Everton strip – was a huge success.

Refusing to be beaten by the creative Mrs Noblett, Old Ma Bushell successfully persuaded the club to let her distribute her Everton Toffees to the fans inside the ground before kick-off. She employed the services of her beautiful grand-daughter Jemima Bushell who, wearing her best hat and dress, went around the ground with a basket full of toffees. So the tradition of the Everton Toffee Lady – which remains to this day – was born.

Tortoise

[athletics] – *the nickname for American Samoan, Trevor Misapeka*

Trevor Misapeka went to the 2001 World Championships in Canada to compete in the shot put, but after a last-minute rule change left him ineligible, he decided to enter the 100 metre sprint instead, in spite of his 21-stone frame. His devastatingly slow 14.28 seconds brought him in over four seconds behind heat-winner Kim Collins. Nevertheless, the amiable Samoan was delighted: 'That's my personal best, I've never run that far before.'

He was affectionately nicknamed Trevor the *Tortoise* and went on to a more appropriate career as a defensive lineman in American football.

total football

[football] – *a system whereby if a player moves out of position, their role is filled by a team-mate, leaving the formation intact*

The term was coined principally to describe the style of play of the great Dutch national side of the 1970s. The strategy required a *total* level of fitness and a gamut of skills from each and every outfield player, as they all had to be able to move to, and play in, each other's positions at any given moment.

I came face to face with *total football* at both club and country level. Playing for Arsenal, I faced the great Ajax who also perfected the system, winning and losing against the Dutch side in European competition. As Scotland goalkeeper, in my second full international appearance and playing against Holland, I was on the losing side, beaten 2-1 in the last minute by the team who went on to become World Cup runners-up in 1974. While Johann Cruyff was the star at executing the system, its mastermind was the brilliant coach/manager, the late Rinus Michels. Otherwise known as *The General* for both his hardline approach as a coach and his famous comment that 'football is war', Michels' success and impact on the game saw him named Coach of the Century by FIFA in 1999.

Triple Crown

[motor racing] – *the unofficial feat of winning the Indianapolis 500, the 24 Hours of Le Mans and the Monaco Grand Prix*

The *Triple Crown* is contested in a number of sports in a number of countries across the world. Some are represented by trophies and some simply by the honour bestowed upon a team for achieving it. Nevertheless, they all take their name from the Triple Crown still contested every year in the Six Nations by England, Ireland, Scotland and Wales. Although the origins of the term are unclear, its first recorded use is thought to have appeared in the following Ireland v Wales match report in the *Irish Times* in 1894:

> *After long years of seemingly hopeless struggle Ireland has achieved the triple crown honours of Rugby foot-ball. For the first time in the annals of the game have the Hibernians proved beyond cavil or doubt their right to be dubbed champions of the nations and that the Irishmen fully deserve the great distinction no one will deny … Hurrah for Hibernia!*

It's thought that it perhaps derived from the 17th-century Triple Crown of King James (*pictured*) – who was King of Scotland as James VI and King of England and King of Ireland as James I – the first King to rule over the three nations (Wales was  considered a part of England at that time).

So although the true derivation of the term is unclear, the fact that the late Graham Hill is the only driver to have completed motorsport's unofficial holy grail isn't, winning the Monaco **Grand Prix** in 1963, 1964, 1965, 1968 and 1969, the Indianapolis 500 in 1966, and the 24 Hours of Le Mans – almost twenty years after his first Monaco win – in 1972. A feat that might never be matched.

Trotters

[football] – *a nickname for Bolton Wanderers FC*

In 1874, a team was formed at Christ Church Sunday school in Bolton. They played their games on the local recreation ground and used the school as their headquarters. They wore red-and-white quartered shirts and became known as the *Reds*. In time the vicar decided he didn't like the church's buildings being used as a meeting point for the football team without his presence and so put a stop to it.

On 28 August 1877, the team got together at the nearby Gladstone Hotel. Having now severed all ties with the Sunday school and consequently homeless, they agreed to call themselves the *Bolton Wanderers*. Although early in their wandering days, it was certainly a prophetic choice as they didn't settle at a permanent home for another eighteen years.

During that time, one of their pitches was next door to a working piggery. In reference to the name of pigs' feet and the frequent necessity for the players to *trot* through the slurry of the pigpens in order to retrieve the ball, they acquired the nickname, *Trotters*.

truck and trailer

[rugby union] – *a form of obstruction*

This is a colloquial term for an illegal move in which two players break off the maul and the *truck* acts as shield for the bound ball-carrying *trailer* behind.

twelfth man

[football] – *a term often used to describe the fans of a team*

There is no doubting the effect of the twelfth man. The home World Cup victories of Uruguay (1930), Italy (1934), England (1966), Germany (1974), Argentina (1978) and France (1998) are no coincidence. A study by *The Times* in 2006 found that in the English Premiership, a home team can be expected to score 37.29 per cent more goals than an away team, this of course due in part to the benefit of the *twelfth man.*

The term originated in Dallas on 2 January 1922, when Texas A&M University were playing defending national champions, Centre College, in the American football Dixie Classic (the forerunner of today's Cotton Bowl). The ferocity of the game and resulting injuries ensured A&M ran out of reserves by the end of the first half. The only eleven remaining fit players were on the pitch. So the coach turned to the stands and from the A&M fans picked out E. King Gill as his possible back-up substitute. Gill agreed so swapped clothes with one of the injured players and stood ready on the touchline throughout the rest of the game. It turned out that there were no further injuries and so Gill was unused. Nevertheless, with his immediate willingness to help under the circumstances, ensured he had already written himself into A&M University folklore. He came to be known as the twelfth man.

After his graduation and subsequent departure from the university, all A&M students, in homage to that day in 1922, would remain standing for the duration of each game their team played as a gesture of their loyalty and readiness to play if asked. Over time, the team's loyal fans, and subsequently the University student body as a whole, also came to be known as the twelfth man.

Over the years, several sports clubs have **retired** the number 12 **shirt** so that they can dedicate it to their fans. These have included Bayern Munich, Torino, Boca Juniors, Feyenoord, and Portsmouth – 'Pompey Fans' being listed as player number 12 on the squad roster printed in each home programme.

Typhoon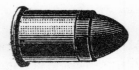

[cricket] – *a nickname for the great Frank Tyson*

In terms of raw, unbridled pace, few bowlers in history come close. Richie Benaud and Don Bradman considered Tyson the quickest they ever saw. In a career plagued and ultimately curtailed by injury, he only played in seventeen Tests, but nevertheless took 76 wickets at an average and strike rate that put him in the ten most effective bowlers in history.

He acquired his nickname during his destruction of the Australian batting line-up on the 1954–55 *Ashes* tour. Having started off with 1 for 160 in defeat at Brisbane, he shortened his run and took ten wickets at Sydney and nine more at

Melbourne. The second innings saw him take 7 for 27 and some still regard it as one of the fastest spells of bowling in cricket history. The MCG curator was even caught illegally watering the pitch at night in an effort to stop it crumbling. The match saw Tyson confirmed *Typhoon*.

But it wasn't just his pace that earned him the name. He was a presence on the pitch, often quoting Shakespeare or Wordsworth to batsmen while out in the middle. In one match, during a hot frustrating afternoon for the England bowlers, Tyson managed to force an outside edge from the batsman that went right through the hands and then legs of Raman Subba Row at first slip. At the end of the over, Subba Row ran over to Tyson and said: 'Sorry, Frank. I should've closed my legs'. Tyson quipped: 'No, you bastard, your mother should have.'

underwear cricket

[cricket] – *Twenty20 cricket*

A disparaging term coined by former Indian opening batsman, Navjot Singh Sidhu, in response to the worldwide spread of the new format of the game and particularly its introduction into Indian cricket's domestic structure. 'If one-day cricket was **pyjama cricket**, then Twenty20 is *underwear cricket*,' remarked Sidhu. 'This cricket is like a burger, you can have it once a week but for a whole meal, you need to return to Test cricket. More than once a week, and it will give you a tummy ache.'

up the jumper

[rugby union] – *a tactic often employed by a team with a strong set of forwards*

This is when a team advances the ball down the pitch through the pack, with little passing and considerable use of the rolling maul. As the ball is often obscured with this style of play and therefore difficult for the defending side to locate, it is as if one of the players has put the ball *up the jumper*.

Valley of Sin

[golf] – *a deep hollow just in front of the 18th green on the Old Course at St Andrews*

This 357-yard, *par*-4 last hole isn't a difficult one, as long as you avoid the *Valley of Sin*. Depending on where the pin has been cut, the drive should usually be aimed at the clock on the Royal and Ancient Clubhouse, setting you up with an approach shot over the Valley. Many people attempt to drive the green in one, and it's this that gives the hollow its name: the notion that they have succumbed to temptation and now find themselves in the Valley of Sin.

Four-time Open champion Tom Morris Snr. designed the green and its adjoining hollow in 1865, and regarded it as his finest work. Apparently, he would often stand and watch with pride players on the green, from the window of his shop just across the street.

Vardon grip

[golf] – *an overlapping grip on the golf club*

This way of holding the club takes its name from the great English champion Harry Vardon (1870–1937). He didn't invent the grip, but as golf's first international celebrity, he certainly popularised it. He was also the first professional golfer to play in knickerbockers, dress shirt, tie and buttoned jacket, and despite his cumbersome attire, he won the Open six times – a record that remains to this day. The credibility that he gave the grip ensured that it's one still used by the vast majority of golfers in today's game. Perhaps we should all reconsider, though, as stars such as Jack Nicklaus and Tiger Woods use the interlocking grip instead.

village

[cricket] – *poor play in professional cricket*

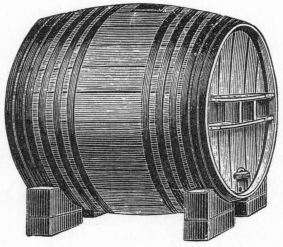

Sometimes used as an adjective to describe the sort of shot, ball or bit of fielding that would find itself more at home on the *village* green than in a seated ground for which people have had to pay to get in.

Wallabies

[rugby union] – *the nickname for the Australian national team*

In 1905, the New Zealand rugby team had made their first tour of Britain and acquired the name **All Blacks** from the British press. In 1908, the Australian rugby team embarked on their first tour of Britain and again, the press felt that the visitors needed a name. Initially, they became the *Rabbits* – but the Australians disliked being called what was to them an imported pest. Instead, they chose and pushed for the native *Wallabies*, which the British press subsequently used.

Originally, only members of touring teams were called Wallabies, but since the 1980s, the name has been used for all players who represent Australia, regardless of whether they play at home or abroad.

War on the Shore

[golf] – *the 1991 **Ryder Cup** played at Kiawah Island in South Carolina, USA*

Like all Ryder Cups, the tension was unbearable, but this time, on the immaculate shores of Kiawah Island and the Atlantic Ocean, it was for all the wrong reasons. In the wake of the first Gulf War on the other side of the world, patriotism ran high, indicated by the terrible decision of Americans Cory Pavin and Steve Pate to play their golf in Desert Storm camouflage caps. The Europeans were not amused when a local radio station launched a 'wake up the enemy' campaign, making calls to their hotel rooms in the early hours. They weren't particularly impressed by the 'welcoming' dinner given in their honour either, which a US PGA official opened by solemnly praying to God for an American victory.

However, it was the action on the course that really started to see the accusations fly. Bernard

Gallacher, the European captain, was convinced that Americans were listening in to his tactical team walkie-talkie transmissions. In the opening four-somes, Seve Ballesteros and José María Olazábal took on Paul Azinger and Chip Beck. On the 7th tee Ballesteros noticed Beck had changed the type of ball the Americans were using. 'I can tell you, we're not trying to cheat', Azinger claimed. 'Oh no. Breaking the rules and cheating are two different things', responded Ballesteros.

When Pate – injured in a car crash before the event – played happily on the second afternoon in his Desert Storm cap but was then withdrawn from the singles due to injury, some wondered if it had been done tactically. The failure of US captain Dave Stockton to tell his European counterpart of the withdrawal and the fact that it automatically secured the Americans a half point by default only served to fuel the accusations that followed.

It all amounted to what the less subtle sectors of the world's media decided to name *The War on the Shore*.

Wednesday

[football] – *an abbreviation of Sheffield Wednesday FC*

On the evening of Wednesday, 4 September 1867, the *Wednesday Cricket Club* met at the Adelphi public house in Sheffield. They took their name from the fact that Wednesday was traditionally the day that the local steel workers who formed the club took their half-day off to play sports. At the meeting, they decided to form a football team so as to keep the cricket side together and fit over the coming winter months. The rest, as they say, is history.

Whispering Death

[cricket] – *the nickname for West Indian fast bowler, Michael Holding*

He was one of the fastest bowlers of his generation, devastating batting line-ups across the world throughout the 1970s and early 80s. His name is perfectly explained by *Wisden*'s Mike Selvey: '[His run] began intimidatingly far away. He turned, and began the most elegant long-striding run of them all, feet kissing the turf silently, his head turning gently and ever so slightly from side to side, rhythmically, like that of a cobra hypnotising its prey. Good batsmen tended not to watch him all the way lest they became mesmerised. To the umpires he was malevolent stealth personified so they christened him *Whispering Death*.'

White Horse Final

[football] – *a name sometimes given to the 1923 FA Cup Final*

Wembley hosted its first final in 1923 having just been completed in under a year at a cost of £750,000. It saw Bolton take on West Ham in what turned out to be perhaps the most famous domestic final of all time. Although capacity for the new stadium was 127,000, the stadium entrances were not finished and so a far higher number of people made it into the ground. No one knows the final number but it's thought it could well have reached a quarter of a million with another 60,000 eventually locked outside.

With thousands having to spill onto the pitch, the game was about to be abandoned (despite the presence of King George V in the Royal Box) when mounted police were called in to push the crowds back to the sides of the playing surface. Among them was PC George Scorey and his famous thirteen-year-old white horse, Billie, who both actually had the day off but had reported for duty as word reached Scorey that the situation in the stadium had got out of hand.

Billie the horse was actually a grey but later appeared bright white in the high-contrast black-and-white newsreel footage and photography of the time. Although a number of other horses were also involved, Billie was the most distinguishable and so, much of the subsequent imagery gave the impression that he had controlled the vast throngs single-handedly. Billie consequently became a legend and the match became known as the White Horse Final.

During the match itself, the vast crowds had caused some fairly unusual moments for an FA Cup Final. When a player stepped up to take a corner or a throw-in, he had to wait while police negotiated him a run-up through the crowd that had formed a human wall around the perimeter of the entire pitch. Early in the first half Bolton's David Jack crashed in a shot hard enough to not only beat West Ham keeper Ted Hutton, but also

to knock a spectator unconscious who was pressed against the net behind the goal. Although the goal was good, it was made somewhat controversial by the fact that West Ham defender Jack Tresadern was still trapped in the crowd after taking the throw-in. In the second half, when Bolton scored their second to secure the Cup, the ball rebounded off the spectators behind the goal and back into play so quickly, that few people realised a goal had been scored. Never again would Wembley see such a vast crowd.

Wizard of the Dribble

[football] – *a nickname for the late great Stanley Matthews*

Sir Stanley Matthews is perhaps the best dribbler of a football the game has ever seen. He won the first ever European Footballer of the Year award, the first Football Writers' Association award, and was the first football player to be knighted for services to sport. His ability to evade a tackle with the ball at his feet was so acute that he was still playing in the top flight when he retired on 6 February 1965, just after his 50th birthday. Even at that age, he always maintained that he retired 'too early'. He was also the perfect gentleman – exemplified by the fact that despite playing in nearly 700 league games, he was never booked.

At 42, he remains the oldest player to have played in an England shirt. His England career is the longest of any player ever to play for the side, stretching from his debut on 29 September 1934 at the age of 19, to his last appearance on 15 May 1957, 23 years later. His international career saw him christened the *Magician* across the world.

Despite all this, arguably his greatest triumph came at Wembley on 2 May 1953 when he brought Blackpool back from 3-1 down with less than twenty minutes to play to beat the Bolton Wanderers 4-3 in the FA Cup Final. Despite his team-mate Stan Mortensen scoring a hat-trick in the game, his display of wizardry with the ball at his feet had such a profound effect on the game that it was subsequently dubbed the *Matthews Final*.

I was fortunate enough to meet Sir Stanley on more than one occasion and now treasure a copy of his autobiography in which he inscribed: 'To my pal Bob. With best wishes, Stan.'

WM

[football] – *a formation featuring five defenders and five attackers – three backs and two halves in defensive roles, and two inside forwards assisting the three attacking forwards*

In 1925 the offside rule was amended so that an attacking player needed only two opponents in front of him and not three as was the case before. This obviously made the offside trap much more difficult to execute and saw the number of goals in the English First Division rise 43 per cent from 1,192 to 1,703 the following year.

In response, the great Herbert Chapman and his Arsenal captain Charles Buchan devised a system whereby the centre-half was pulled back in to a centre-back role in order to deal with the now more dangerous and prolific centre forward. To fill up the gap created in midfield, the two inside forwards were pulled back to create a four-man midfield, or *magic square* as it would later become known. When all was said and done, the general shape of the defensive players made up a *W* and the attacking players, an *M* – a formation that became known as the *WM*.

yellow jersey

[cycling] – *the jersey worn by the overall leader of the Tour de France*

The Tour de France was founded as a marketing stunt for a French newspaper called *L'Auto*, by its editor and co-founder, Henri Desgrange, back in 1902. Held annually, the race, and consequently the circulation of *L'Auto*, went from strength to strength. During the 1919 Tour, on the rest day in Luchon, it occurred to Desgrange that the race leader should wear something distinctive to ensure all spectators knew who was winning. On 10 July 1919, he announced that it was to be a *yellow jersey*, a decision he had reached because of the yellow paper *L'Auto* was printed on. Mercantile as it was, he had created one of the most famous icons in sport.

yips

[golf] – *a psychological syndrome that affects a golfer's technique, especially when putting*

This mental affliction can profoundly affect a golfer's career. A head-on collision with a Greyhound bus nearly brought the great Ben Hogan's career to an end, but it didn't. The *yips* did. The term was conceived over 70 years ago by another sufferer – the Open, US Open and USPGA winner Tommy Armour. He used 'yips' to describe 'that ghastly time when with the first movement of the putter, the golfer blacks out, loses sight of the ball and hasn't the remotest idea of what to do with the putter or, occasionally, that he is holding a putter at all'.

There are similar afflictions in other sports, notably darts, in which players can totally lose control of the dart they are throwing, and in more severe cases can't let go of the dart at all. This is known as *dartitis* and its most famous sufferer was five-times World Champion, Eric Bristow.

yorker

[cricket] – *a delivery that pitches on the popping crease*

This is a very difficult ball for a batsman to play. It's most usually and successfully deployed sparingly as a surprise weapon, often being executed as a slower ball. The aim of the *yorker* is to deceive the batsman in the flight. As a result, it takes its name from the 18th-century colloquialism to *york* or to *pull yorkshire* on someone, meaning to trick or mislead.

Australians call it a *sandshoe crusher* or a *toe crusher*.

Yo-Yos

[football] – *a nickname for Stirling Albion FC*

Stirling Albion had a reputation in the past of always being too good for one division but never quite good enough for the one above. In the 1950s they were promoted and relegated seven times, inspiring the saying in Scotland that somebody or something 'goes up and down like Stirling Albion'. The club's fans decided to make light of their predicament and so named their team the *Yo-Yos*.

Zebras

[football] – *a nickname for Juventus FC*

Juventus FC was founded on 1 November 1897, by a group of boys aged between fourteen and seventeen. They played in pink shirts because it was the cheapest material available. Although the club grew quickly, entering the Italian Football Championship in 1900, they continued to use their pink shirts. However, as the number of games increased, so did the need to wash the shirts and they faded too quickly. So in 1903 the club decided to find a new kit. John Savage, an English player at the club at the time asked his friend to send over some shirts from England. His friend, being an ardent Notts County fan, sent a set of his beloved team's black-and-white striped shirts to Turin. Juventus have worn them ever since, becoming the *Zebras*.

zooter

[cricket] – *a delivery by a leg-spinner, slipped out of the hand with little or no spin on it, but which dips in to the batsman late in flight*

The name for this delivery was introduced by Shane Warne and his bowling coach and mentor, Terry Jenner. Some think they gave it a name so it could be added to the list of other named deliveries in his arsenal such as the *flipper* and *slider*, just to enhance his aura of mystery, and consequently to create more doubt in a batsman's mind as to what they will face when he bowls.

There is no doubt that Warne is one of the greatest bowlers the world has ever seen, but spin in the non-cricketing sense (according to the motto that all publicity is good publicity) has also always been a strength of his, and this is part of his appeal. A drugs ban, the ***Ball of the Century***, a record number of Test wickets, and tabloid scandals on the front and back pages have all added to the media frenzy surrounding Warne – assigning him sufficient celebrity to earn the nickname *Hollywood*.

Index